Tips for Toddlers

Also by Brooke McKamy Beebe
Best Bets for Babies

Tips for Toddlers

Time-saving, trouble-saving,
money-saving tips for those terrific twos
and threes from the real experts—
parents.

Brooke McKamy Beebe

with illustrations by Denise Cavalieri Fike

REVISED EDITION

Delta

The tips in this book have all worked for the parents who submitted them. Children are individuals, however, and not all tips will be suitable for you and your child. If you have any questions at all, please check with your doctor. The author and publisher advise you to use your common sense and your intimate knowledge of your own child. We cannot be held responsible for the misuse of any information in this book.

A DELTA BOOK
Published by
Dell Publishing
a division of
Bantam Doubleday Dell Publishing Group, Inc.
666 Fifth Avenue
New York, New York 10103

Library of Congress Cataloging in Publication Data

Beebe, Brooke M.
    Tips for toddlers : time-saving, trouble-saving, money-saving tips for those terrific twos and threes from the real experts— parents / Brooke McKamy Beebe ; with illustrations by Denise Cavalieri Fike.—Rev. ed.
        p.   cm.
    Includes index.
    ISBN 0-385-30834-5 (pbk.)
    1. Child rearing.   2. Toddlers.   I. Title.
HQ774.5.B43   1993
649'.1—dc20   92-17447
                                                        CIP

Manufactured in the United States of America
Published simultaneously in Canada
January 1993
10 9 8 7 6 5 4 3 2 1

*To all the parents
who contributed their ideas
so generously*

Contents

Preface to the Revised Edition

Since this book was originally published, I've received many hundreds of letters containing terrific new tips as well as thoughtful suggestions for improving the book. All the good tips and improvements have been incorporated in this revised, expanded edition. I am deeply grateful to the many parents who wrote to me over the years, offering their tips, knowledge, enthusiasm, concerns, and even photographs. Now I can share their wisdom with you.

In addition, this revised edition would not have been possible without the interest, enthusiasm and sage advice of both Emily Reichert, my editor at Delta, and Heide Lange, my agent. Once again Dr. Rose Ames has given generously of her time and expertise to check the "Health" and "Safety" sections and has patiently answered many questions. Beth Pollack has contributed great ideas and tips of her own as well as updated information throughout the book, and Sally Ziegler, executive director of the Child Care Council of Westchester, gave wise counsel generally as well as specifically on child care. Dr. Bob Seaver generously shared his psychiatric expertise with me, and Dr. Robert Koweek helped to polish the section on dental care. Dr. Lewis Goldfrank, medical director of the New York City Poison Control Center, supplied up-to-date information on poisons, poisonous plants and safety issues. Jean Grasso Fitzpatrick, author of *Something More: Nurturing Your Child's Spiritual Growth*, and Iris VanderPutten were always available for professional and personal advice and support. My most sincere thanks and appreciation to all.

Acknowledgments

I'm deeply grateful to the original editor, Cynthia Vartan, for her excellent counsel and contributions; to Judy Newman, publicist *extraordinaire;* to Lisa Heila Clemmens for her editorial assistance; to Cynthia Boyd, Holly Lachowicz, Dorleau Roth, Linda Rutledge, Renata Rutledge and Sue Stevenson for their help in finding parents in various parts of the country to respond to my questionnaire; to Connie Bannon, Pat Brosnan, Rosemary Capozza, Kathie duQuesnay, Dorothy Hayes, Marilyn Markowitz, Yvonne Pollack and Jean Sparacin for their careful reading of various parts of the manuscript and valuable suggestions; to Sally Dow, Children's Librarian, Ossining Public Library, for her reading recommendations; and to Tyler, Scott and Drew, my husband and sons, for their love and understanding.

In addition, I would like to thank Edward Krenzelok, director of the Hennepin Regional Poison Center and associate professor, College of Pharmacy, University of Minnesota, and the Hudson Valley Poison Control Center at Nyack Hospital for checking and adding to the information on poisons, and Barbara Tursky, program coordinator for the Westchester County Traffic Safety Board, for her advice on car-seat safety.

I'm very grateful to the following radio stations that allowed me to gather tips for toddlers from their audiences: KGNR, Sacramento, California; WINZ, Miami, Florida; WIFE, Indianapolis, Indiana; WOC, Davenport, Iowa; WFDF, Flint,

Michigan; KTOK, Oklahoma City, Oklahoma; KLBJ, Austin, Texas; and WOAI, San Antonio, Texas.

And most especially I would like to thank all the people in the following list, who gave so unstintingly of their time, energy and experiences. The book was written by them and for you.

Jane Abel
Augustine A. Arena
Mary Helen Arena
Roberta Arnold
Connie Bannon
Randy Banter
Nancy Barber
Ron Barber
Janet Barnes
Janis Baron
Edward Barticciotto
Sheila Barticciotto
Claudia Benvenuto
Susan Berenzweig
Pat Berkery
Tara Billings
Maggie Bitencourt
Linda Blacker
Marj Bleier
Joan Boardman
Rebecca Bohannon
Donna Bonanno
John Bonanno
Cindy Bowles
John Boyle
Patricia Boyle
Mary Bronnimann
Patricia Brosnan
Linda Bryan
Steve Bryan
Anna Byrnes
Kevin Byrnes

Patricia S. Cable
Joseph Capozza
Rosemary Capozza
Cynthia Carlaw
Molly Castner
Ronnie Chernick
Sandy Choron
Jan Christopherson
Phyllis Cohn
Judy Collmer
Gerry Colombraro
Jane Comings
Susan Court
Paul Courtman
Cathy Daly
Marilee Davis
Susan Decker-Bunce
Patricia DeGregorie
Pamela Dey
Marcia Dillon
Carol DiRaffaele
Gary DiRaffaele
Susan Dodd
Cherie Dunham
Kathie duQuesnay
Elaine Eisenman
John Erwin
Marlen Erwin
Alice Faribault
Rosanne M. Ferris
Larry Finer
Sheila Finer

Laura Lee Fiore
Ralph A. Fiore
Jeannie Fitzpatrick
Barbara Fitzsimmons
Holly Foster
Lucy Fowler
John Franchi
Linda Franchi
Albert Andrew
    French
Debora Taylor
    French
Evelyn Fyler
Mrs. John Gavlik
Sharon Gendron
Fred Giampino
Lorraine Giampino
Nancy M. Gottlieb
Sandy Grant
Micki Greiner
Henry Gross II
Nancy Weiser Gross
Barbara Hamill
John Hamill
Joan W. Hanley
Bonnie Harlow
Eleanor Harvey
Dorothy Hayes
Loretta Haynes
Lucy Head
Martha E.
    Hendricks

Judy Hogan
Chris Hovey
Renee L. Huettl
Suzanne T. Isaacs
Lori Jacobs
Carol Jaconetti
Angie Jasinski
Jim Jasinski
Madeline Jones
Daniel Kaden
Melissa Kaden
Virginia Kahrs
Kathleen Kane-
   Molito
Kelly Karahalios
Ed Kardouskas
Fran Kardouskas
Faith Kelly
Suzann Kettler
Louisa Kimball
Kathy Kirtley
Julie Konopa
Robert A. Koweek,
   D.M.D.
Edward Krenzelok
Bridget Krowe
Elliot Krowe
Raynell Kubatska
Barbara Kuczen
Wendy Kuhlwein
Audrey Kuntz
Marcia Kunz
Theresa Kwiecinski
Charles La Clare
Jean La Clare
Mary Laidlaw
Lori LaManna
Pamela Landolt
Heide Lange
Janet Lanzilloto
John Lanzilloto

Robert F. Lawrence,
   Jr.
Sheryl T. Lawrence
Mark Lindemann
Vivian Lindemann
Barbara Lutkenhaus
Wayne Lutkenhaus
Bill Mackintosh
Liz Macwhinnie
Nancy Maher
Myrna Malave-
   Stoiber
Debra Manette
Joanne L. Mangusi
John Mangusi
Marilyn Markowitz
Laura Mason
JoAnn Matthews
Michael Matthews
Marilyn May
Sherry Mazer
Joan McCormick
Josephine
   McDermott
Karen McFadden
Carol Anne McGrath
Harold R. McGrath
Lori McHugh
Linda McInvale
Bill McKamy
Steve McKamy
Rochelle McKinney
Lynda McMillan
Dorothy M. Meighan
William F. Meighan
Patricia Meudt
Elizabeth Miller
Margaret Miller
Barbara Mitchell
Mary Ann Moore
Sandra Moore

Susan Morettini
Karen Muller
Marilyn Mullins
Rosalie Murray
Joan Neale
Celeste Odierna
Glen Owen
Linda Owen
John Palkowitsch
Lisa Palkowitsch
Eileen Roth Paroff
Harvey Paroff
Louise Pauzano
Jill Pedersen
Mark Phelan
Maryellen Phelan
Janet Piccolo
Nicholas Piccolo
Ginnie Piechocniski
Lenny Piechocniski
Max Plesset
Tina Plesset
Kimberly Plummer
Beth Pollack
Yvonne Pollack
Stephen G. Posniak
Terrilynn M.
   Quillen, R.N.
Ellen Reppucci
Suzan Resnick
Monica Restaino
Lennie Richards
Kathie Rigano
Richard Rigano
Kathie Roberts
Sandy Robson
Bunny Roosevelt
Beth Rose
Hannah Ross
Dorleau Roth
Linda Rutledge

Renata Rutledge
Teresa Salanitro
Maggie Sarno
Marie Savanella
Cynthia Schein
Robin Schultz
Robert I. Seaver,
    M.D.
Esther Schulder
William Schulder
Doreen Semel
Lucretia Shapiro
Donna Sherwood
Jonette Shuja
Grace Siciliano
John Siciliano
Elizabeth Silverman
Maria Smacchia
Nick Smacchia
Susan Smith
Jill Smoot
Lisa Sokal

Yonatan Sokal,
    M.D.
Albert F.
    Sonnberger
Dorothy Sonnberger
Jean Sparacin
Balli Spear
Olga Speck
Marjorie Stephens
Laurie Sterlacci
Sue Stevenson
Allison Stewart
Barbara O. Strang
Marjorie Strauss
Larry Strulowitz
Sheila Strulowitz
Marilyn Sullivan
John K. Tanner
Nancy B. Tanner
Jayne B. Taylor
Warren Thomas
Janice Tonkin

Pam Torborg
Susan Ulmer
Valerie Urban
Judy Vaillancourt
Gerry Van Dusen
Carolyn Vaughn
Henry R. Voelker
Susan Voelker
Anita L. Walsh
George J. Walsh III
Isabella Watson
Laurie Williams
Taylor Williamson
Susan Willoughby
Dorothy Wolf
Lisa Wolf
Sally Elizabeth
    Wolfson
Nadine Ziegler
Sally Ziegler
Deborah Zucconi
Fred Zucconi

Introduction

As I finished my first book, *Best Bets for Babies*, my son Scott was rocketing through his third year, throwing temper tantrums, needing to be toilet trained and doing all those delightful and terrible things we associate with the twos and threes. I needed help! I'd just amassed hundreds of tips for babies, but where were the tips for twos and threes? Certainly these years demand skilled and creative parenting, too. So I went right back to collecting tips again, and the result is *Tips for Toddlers*. It contains ideas, suggestions and advice for parents of children two and three years old.

In these important years a child changes from an irrational, demanding baby to a relatively reasonable, civilized human being—if, that is, his or her parents can survive the challenge of the civilizing process. It's easy to deal with babies' problems in a physical way by distracting them or simply removing them from difficult situations. But toddlers demand new skills from us. No longer are they so easily distracted. We must cope with their growing understanding, verbal skills and strong desire for control. Now they know what they want and are determined to get it.

It is helpful for parents to know that the negative behavior exhibited by most children of this age is not only normal but necessary to their growth and development. They must separate from their parents, find their own limits, learn to control their emotions, deal with fears and frustrations. It's a tall order for such little people. However, we parents do not always feel sympathetic and understanding; it's hard to be patient or kindly in the midst of a raging tantrum or when you hear "no" for the thousandth time. At that point *we* need help. And the best help comes from other mothers and fathers who have gone through it all and have found some techniques that work.

So that is what you'll find in this book: practical suggestions and advice from other parents about coping creatively with two- and three-year-old children. I collected these ideas from friends and friends of friends and sent hundreds of questionnaires to parents all over the country. When I did radio and television shows, many parents in the audience had great tips to offer. All these people have shared with me the tips that have worked for them, and I hope they will work for you.

Naturally each child is different, and what works for one may not work for another. That's why I've included a range of ideas, some of which are even contradictory and some of which you may disagree with. If you do, fine! We all should have our own personal parenting styles. Select those ideas that seem good for you and your child and try them out. You may be surprised, as I was, by how many little things there are that can make these years so much easier and happier.

The tips are short and arranged by subject so that you can find the information you need quickly. I know parents of toddlers don't have a minute to spare! You might want to check off the tips that worked best for you for future reference or to pass along to friends. And I hope you will pass along to me any of your own ideas that you've found effective for your children. I have been delighted with the response from the readers of the first edition of *Tips for Toddlers*, and

I hope you will be just as generous. Please be part of this growing network of parents who are sharing with other parents their ideas that *really work*!

Brooke

Brooke

P.S. If you'd like to share your tips, ideas and/or suggestions with me, I'd be delighted to receive them.
Just write to:
Brooke McKamy Beebe
Tips for Toddlers
℅ Dell Publishing
666 Fifth Avenue
New York, NY 10103

If we use your tip(s) in the next edition of *Tips for Toddlers*, we'll send you a free copy of the book. Please share your tips with me (with the understanding that I have permission to use what you send in any edition), and join our network of parents.

1

Growing Up

It's probably hard for you to believe that your helpless baby has changed so quickly into such an independent little person. But growing up is not easy—for the child or the parent! Your two- and three-year-old will amaze you with rapid mastery of language and movement, then appall you by suddenly reverting to infantile behavior. As one of my contributors advised: *"Anticipate moves toward independence and also anticipate (and try not to be disappointed by) regressions. They are normal. It's difficult to give up all the things associated with babyhood at once."*

This chapter deals mostly with the difficult stages of growth most children must go through according to their own unique timetable of development in order to mature into happy, healthy adults. It's comforting to realize that this behavior is normal and necessary; it's also nice to know that your child will grow out of it!

Negative Behavior

The negative behavior common at this stage can be really tough to live through, even when you know it signals a positive move toward independence. Do read some books about children's development and behavior to help you understand the reasons for your child's negativism.

The following tips will help you cope on a day-to-day basis:

☑ Never ask a two-year-old if he wants to do something. The answer will be "No." Instead say "We're going to the store now."

☐ Offering limited choices distracts the child from what you want him to do. Say "Do you want to wear mittens or the gloves?" or "Who are you bringing to the car, Ernie or Bert?" But don't give choices when it matters.

☐ At some point it seems as if all you say to your child is "No!" even if you've baby-proofed your house so well you can hardly live in it. Figure out some *positive* things to say instead, such as "Hot", "Pet the cat *this* way," "Share your toys," "Spit it out—it tastes bad!" This way of speaking does not come naturally, by the way. It's learned behavior.

☑ If your child is constantly answering you with negative replies such as "No," "Just a minute," or "Not now," try listening to yourself for a while. Is your child giving you back your own words?

☐ You will be more relaxed if you change your habits and allow *more time* to get anywhere, do anything. This allows gentle persuasion to have an effect. Often the more you push the child to hurry, the slower he goes.

☐ Change roles so your child doesn't have Mommy or Daddy to resist. For example, pretend to be Grandad when dressing your child, bring a puppet to the dinner table and have *her* discuss mealtime behavior, or pretend you are the child's best friend at bedtime. Playacting diverts, distracts and amuses both of you, and if you listen carefully, you'll learn a lot about your child's feelings.

☐ Tell your child stories of your own childhood and how *you* hated to have your hair brushed, or whatever. Emphasize how much better she is than you were.

☐ Tell your child stories of how he resisted various things (diapering, shampooing, etc.) as a baby. Emphasize how grown up he is now that he does all these things without a fuss.

☐ It's surprising how well reverse psychology can work if used in a humorous way, for example, "Don't wash your hands before lunch today!" Naturally your child must understand the joke. You don't want to confuse reverse psychology with real instructions, but many children will understand and enjoy the game.

☐ When faced with a real pout, say "Don't laugh. Now no laughs. I don't want to hear one giggle."

☐ *"I don't think enough can be said for a change of scene. A short walk in the mall or 15 minutes outdoors even in bad weather can change the course of a whole day. On her way to work, a neighbor once remarked about how nice it must be to be out strolling with two toddlers and a cup of coffee. Little did she know that they both had been crying since before breakfast."*

☐ Transitions, especially departures, are difficult at this age. To ease a small guest out the door without tears, keep a few inexpensive toys or sugarless lollipops by the door. When saying good-bye, give one to the guest and one to your child.

☐ A sense of humor goes a long way to ward off or stop whining. *"My husband invented invisible bugs called 'grumpies.' When whining begins, he makes a big production out of finding grumpies up our daughter's sleeves, in her hair, under her shoes. By the time he's found four or five, the whining cycle has been broken."*

☐ If your child is refusing to let you change his diapers, tell him that his dog (cat, guinea pig, etc.) won't want to play if he has "poopy pants!" This usually brings giggles and cooperation. (For more tips on changing and dressing, see pages 101–104.)

☐ If your child is whining to be held while shopping, find a place to rest and recharge. Then bring out a pull toy and say "Why don't you take turtle for a walk?" In other words, supply some motivation.

☐ Next time your child is cranky in a store, think: How would you feel if a giant held your hand over your head and pulled you here and there?

☐ Games can often get you through shopping and doing errands with a cranky child. Let your child hold the coupons and match pictures with products. Let him guess how long each errand will take and time it. Guess how many children will be in the next store. Find an empty aisle in the supermarket, give your cart (with the child in it) a gentle push and let go. Wave bye-bye. This really tickles children. Just be careful not to push the cart into a stack of cans!

☐ Your child will be much happier doing errands with you if you promise a "time" treat, such as 10 minutes in the toy department or 20 minutes on the swings after you're through.

☐ As an alternative to saying "No," pretend to read signs outside of the stores and restaurants your child is begging to invade. Those signs might say "No children under six allowed," or "The pizza ovens are broken." You could probably find a "sign" on a candy machine that says it's "out of order."

☐ To get a reluctant child going, put your hand on his back and push *gently* as you talk about what you're going to see or do.

☐ To stop a series of "whys," give your child a clear explanation, then ask her to repeat it back to you, explaining that you want to make sure she understands it. This works best with a three.

☐ Give warnings before you interrupt playing to change or dress your child. Try saying something like "I need to change your diaper. Let's count to 10 first."

☐ Reluctance to anything can often be overcome if you initiate a race—"I bet I can beat you," or "Let's see who gets there first." This game—and its variations—works very well when you meet daily resistance to the same thing. One mother reports: *"Our son used to be reluctant to go to the bathroom at night so his father could brush his teeth, but this technique worked: I would 'fool' his daddy by saying something like 'Oh, look at this picture in the paper, Dad,' and then whisper to my son to run quickly into the bathroom to beat his daddy. Of course his dad made a big to-do about the race to the bathroom. Once they were both in there, there was no problem."*

☐ When your toddler wants something (a cookie, trip to the playground) that she can't have at that time, satisfy the desire by pretending. For example, say "We can't eat real cookies now. Can you find some pretend ones?" Be sure to "gobble" them up with your child.

☐ If you're in no mood for games, give the child a choice of two alternatives ("Would you like to go to your room or get your boots on?"), and she will probably pick the lesser of two evils.

☐ Remember, if you give a child a choice, she will probably pick the second simply because it's mentioned last. If you have a preference, it's wise to put it last.

☐ And then there's always the counting routine as a last resort: "If you're not out the door by the time I count to five, I'll . . ." You supply the motivator, but if you're disobeyed you *must* do what it was you said you'd do. (This has fairly limited success with the twos; it's more effective as your child grows older.)

☐ Try an indoor slide or climbing frame to work off the excess energy that can turn into negative behavior.

☐ Negative behavior might be a signal that you need to spend more time alone with your child. Perhaps he's trying to provoke you into giving him some attention.

☐ Do not rule out sickness. For example, cranky children who sleep well, eat well and don't pull on their ears can still have an ear infection. Check it out.

☐ Unless you want hassles all day long, decide what things you're going to insist on (anything that involves your child's safety, for example) and relax about the other stuff. In other words, choose your battles.

☐ Try to anticipate stressful times and plan for them. When you're stressed, you can't think straight, so do your planning and thinking when you're relaxed.

☐ The time before dinner is not called "arsenic hour" for nothing. Many parents let their children play in the kitchen sink at this time. Others pull out a special art box. This is the time for the child's favorite activity.

☐ Always state the rules and limits you've decided on loud and clear *before* rules are broken and limits are reached. It is, however, a fact of this stage that the child will test rules (and you).

☐ Negative behavior *is* a stage; some children just have to test you every hour of every day. This *will* pass! Take two aspirin, get a good night's sleep and remind yourself that four is a lovely age.

Temper Tantrums

Tantrums usually occur when children are hungry and/or tired. If your child is having them frequently, check your child's schedule carefully. By providing lunch/snack/dinner earlier, you may prevent most tantrums. For instance, a child who often has tantrums at 5 P.M. may just need dinner at that time.

As children begin to give up naps, their energy levels change. Early bedtime or an afternoon quiet time may be necessary to avoid fatigue.

Frustration is frequently a primary cause of tantrums. A rapidly growing two-year-old often wants to do more than his physical capabilities allow, and as yet he has no way to cope with his lack of ability. Parents need to be very sensitive to this and to try to step in to help before tremendous frustration occurs. Of course, some frustration is crucial to learning; a child *needs* to be challenged and learn to handle frustration.

Speaking of challenges, dealing with tantrums is one of the most challenging aspects of parenting. Good luck!

☐ BE CALM! This is hard, but a parent's anger or frustration can really escalate the force of the tantrum. Never scream at or hit a child who is having a temper tantrum. It will not help and will just upset the child even more.

☐ Pick the child up and hug her when you see tension building (and even if you don't). *"My daughter was really jealous of the baby, and these extra hugs did—and still do—the trick."*

☐ Without any anger, remove the child to a quiet place. Tell her when she stops crying (kicking, biting, hitting) she is welcome back. When she returns, talk about (1) what happened, (2) how it could have been prevented. Children have to learn to control or channel their frustrations, and it is up to us to teach them. If the tantrum resumes, repeat the isolation technique.

☐ If a hysterically crying child is unable to catch her breath, simply blow air in her face, as if you were blowing out a candle. A reflex reaction causes the child to inhale.

☐ Sometimes music is calming. A cassette or record player gives a child something to focus on, too.

☐ Change the environment to make it less stressful for your child (and you). Is there something that always drives him crazy? Can you figure out how to eliminate that stress?

☐ Some children respond well to the suggestion "Go to your room and find a happy face before you come out."

☐ Don't listen or react to anything while she's screaming. Make sure she understands that the way to get your attention is by talking, not screaming.

☐ Carry healthful snacks with you at all times. Rice cakes, raisins, dried fruit, crackers and fruit juice in cans or bottles are very portable, and it's easy to grab a piece of fresh fruit as you leave the house. Rapid growth often leaves children hungrier than you might expect, and a banana just might divert that hunger-caused tantrum.

☐ Get a punching bag. Let your child hit it when he's angry, and he may let off enough steam to avoid a full-fledged tantrum.

☐ *"My son used to lie facedown on the kitchen floor and kick his feet. One day I simply took off his shoes. No more noise, and it hurt his little toes. After that, no more tantrums."*

☐ If the tantrum is about something denied (such as candy), *don't* give in to stop it. If the child gets what she wants by throwing a tantrum, she quickly learns that tantrums work and will have many more.

☐ Ignore the tantrum. If you can't stand the howling, go somewhere else and do something physical and noisy, such as carpentry or vacuuming.

☐ A hysterical child might be soothed by a cool washcloth dabbed on her face.

☐ Have a (pretend) tantrum yourself. Your child will see how silly it looks and stop.

☐ Just say "If you want to cry, cry." It tends to take the wind out of children's sails. Or tell the child to yell louder or cry harder.

☐ If you're in a store, calmly take your child outside or to the car. When the crying is over, go back and finish what you were doing. You don't want her to learn she can stop you from shopping by having a tantrum.

☐ If your child is having a real spate of tantrums, try this: Just when one begins, gather the child in your arms and hold tightly until the tantrum has run its course. It will be very unpleasant for you, but as one mother reports, *"I can't explain it, but holding Jeremy during a tantrum seemed to put him back together and really calmed him down for weeks."*

☐ Whisper interesting things into her ear, such as all the fun she can have playing when she stops crying. Or begin a story. She may stop crying in order to hear you.

☐ Make sure the tantrums aren't bids for attention. If you suspect this, spend more time one-to-one with your child and see if it helps. Remember, reward good behavior with your attention.

☐ Sometimes children deliberately pick fights with you; they're testing their limits. So put your foot down, let the tears and screams come, and then the tantrum will (it's hoped) be over.

☐ It's hard not to feel victimized by a child who seems to be intent on driving you crazy. As one parent puts it, *"Try to remember that you are dealing with a child, your child, and not some big, ugly monster who is out to get you."* Release your anger—*away* from your child—but release it.

☐ The best investment in your mental health you may ever make is to hire a baby-sitter to give you some time away from your child during difficult periods.

☐ If you feel your feelings of anger and frustration are sometimes more than you can handle, if you've hurt or want to hurt your child, call Parents Anonymous at this toll-free number: (800) 421-0353 (for California residents: [800] 352-0386). Emergency consultation is available, and you will be referred to a local PA self-help association.

Discipline

Naturally you will adjust your disciplinary measures to the age and temperament of your child. Five minutes of crib confinement may be all that's necessary to discipline a two-year-old. Don't forget that twos do forget rules quickly and need many reminders. A three-year-old is much more aware of behavior and its consequences.

GENERAL OBSERVATIONS

☐ Always remember to praise and reward *good* behavior at every opportunity. This is the best discipline you could ever use. *"A good day rates a gold star on our calendar,"* reports one parent. *"Five gold stars means a special treat."*

☐ Children generally misbehave when they are hungry, tired or bored. Always carry small snacks with you, as well as toys, books or crayons to occupy them in restaurants, waiting rooms, and the like.

☐ Getting angry doesn't help.

☐ Be prepared to repeat your rules endlessly.

☐ Decide on your method of discipline in advance. Warn your child of the consequences of particular actions and *follow through*.

☐ Don't ever use a threat if you can't carry it out. *"I used to threaten I'd leave my child home if she didn't cooperate and get dressed. It worked until one day when she called my bluff and I was really stuck. We had to go that day."*

☐ Discipline must be consistent and fair for it to be effective.

☐ All you may really need to do is adjust the environment to your child. For example, he won't rip up your magazines if they're kept out of reach.

☐ Before you discipline for bad behavior, try to find out the cause. *"I caught my son hammering a nail into the arm of a chair and sent him to his room. After about ten minutes I went to talk to him about what he had done. He told me that he saw his grandpa hammering a nail into a chair the other day and he thought it was all right. I explained the difference between the two acts, and I apologized for my misunderstanding. There is usually a good reason why children do what they do."*

☐ Discipline should be immediate. If a child misbehaves

in the morning, don't wait till the evening to discipline her.

☐ Give adequate warning if you're going to punish a child for a specific behavior. For example, if the child has been biting and suddenly, in anger, you punish him, he may not really connect the punishment with the crime. Give fair warning ("Do that once more and you'll have to sit on the stairs"), *repeat* the warning, make the child repeat it, then *follow through* if the child bites. This usually does the trick.

☐ To avoid arguments, have some rules, such as those regarding bedtime or after-dinner snacks, that are simply nonnegotiable.

☐ If the child has done something unacceptable, it does not hurt, even after your initial discipline, to discuss the incident with your spouse within the child's earshot. Sometimes your reasoning sinks in better when it is not spoken directly to the child in moments of anger or frustration.

☐ When your child is being impossible, try saying to him "You're making me very angry now. If you don't stop by the time I count to three, I'll be very, *very* angry." If he stops, you can both cool down. Children don't usually want their parents mad at them. If he continues, at least he has had fair warning. And sometimes after *you* blow off a little steam, things calm down. A good follow-up is a kiss and a hug to make you both feel better. Then you can have a discussion of *why* whatever happened made you angry. Have the child tell *you*.

☐ Because children are great imitators, observe their play with dolls or animals. If they're scolding and spanking a lot, they may be telling you something about your own behavior toward them.

☐ If you're not having much luck with disciplinary measures, ask at your child's nursery school (day-care center, etc.) what measures they use. Your child may respond better to that method.

METHODS OF DISCIPLINE

For Two-Year-Olds

Choose your battles carefully. Remember, you can't expect a two to be perfect. Not one of them is. (Are you?) But every child needs limits—and will *test* them. Here are some specific ways parents cope with rule breaking:

☐ Physically remove the child from the source of the problem. Do not allow her to continue what she was doing until she cooperates.

☐ Make him sit in a special chair, on a stair step or in a corner for two to five minutes. (Choosing a corner for punishment will at least give you a place to send a child if misbehavior occurs away from home.) Five minutes may not seem long to you, but it's an eternity to a young child. Set the timer. Remind him why he was punished and give him a hug when it's over.

☐ If a child won't sit in a chair (many twos won't stay put), put her in the crib or a more confined space for a short time.

☐ Take away a toy the child loves for the rest of the day. Give it back in the morning with a reminder about why you took it away.

☐ Don't allow some favorite activity for the rest of the morning or afternoon.

For Three-Year-Olds

All the suggestions for twos apply to threes, but the most-often-mentioned discipline for threes was sending them to their rooms.

☐ Sending the child to his room gets him out of your hair and gives him a chance to calm down by himself.

☐ Some parents set a timer, which will signal when the child can come out of her room; others don't want a child to reappear until she can be pleasant again.

☐ *"My three-year-old, who is hyperactive, had great difficulty calming himself down after being punished for misbehavior. I finally found a solution: I set up a fish tank in his room and told him to watch it when he was angry or upset. The difference was amazing! It calms him right down."*

For More Information

☐ To request a free reprint of the article "Positive Discipline," call the ERIC Clearinghouse on Elementary and Early Childhood Education at (217) 333-1386 or send a self-addressed, stamped envelope to: ERIC/EECE, 805 West Pennsylvania Ave., Urbana, IL 61801.

Self-Esteem

One of our obligations as parents is to make our children feel good about themselves. Here are some ideas to think about:

☐ Don't be afraid to lavish praise on your children for all the wonderful things they do, from identifying letters to kissing the baby.

☐ Tell them how much more self-control (or whatever) they have now than they did a few months ago.

☐ Don't compare your children to friends or to each other. Each child follows a unique timetable of development.

☐ Expect regression at certain times (arrival of a new baby, moving, any big change). Don't harp on the babyish behavior; instead, concentrate on the "grown-up" way to do things.

☐ Before you say no to something that looks dangerous, watch and see what the child's capabilities are. One father reports, *"My son was fascinated with stepladders, and since we were painting, they were around a lot (the three-foot kind). When he started to climb up, I just let him but stood close by in case he lost his balance. Even though he was just two, he was very careful and enormously proud of his accomplishment. His grandmother almost had a heart attack when she saw him do it, but we assured her that he had learned how by himself and it was safe."* (Needless to say, an adult should always be present when such activities are taking place, and the child must understand this.)

☐ If you find your child growing fearful and timid around more aggressive children, teach her to shout at anyone who is bullying or threatening. A loud, forceful "No!" or "Go away!" has been known to intimidate many aggressive children. You will probably have to role-play this behavior many times with your child; she will love shouting "no" to you! Also, role-play with her just before she is going to see one of her aggressive friends.

☐ If your child draws something really special, transfer the design to a plain pillow with permanent markers. You could also appliqué it or embroider it. Be sure to put the child's name and the date on it.

☐ If you have a very aggressive child, you probably spend most of your time dragging him away from other kids. Here's an idea: Seek out friends for him who are older and tougher. Your child will soon begin to change his ways when his bullying is not tolerated.

☐ Toddlers will always get into mischief and make you angry, but remember to remind them verbally that even though you're angry, you still love them. Besides being important for their self-esteem, it will make you feel better later if you suspect you've gone overboard in your anger, as we all do from time to time.

☐ Separate the deed from the person—that is, what the child did was wrong, but remind her that she herself is a good, lovable person.

☐ *"Every day we have a family hug where we huddle to-*

gether and hug and kiss each member of the family. This just makes us feel terrific about ourselves and each other."

Breaking Habits

BITING

There are many reasons why toddlers bite others. Biting hard can feel good, and toddlers love to experiment. Biting can also be a reaction to tension or frustration. Most toddlers cannot express their feelings verbally yet, and many resort to biting as a means of expression. Try to discover the reason for the biting. For example, if the child is teething, provide acceptable chewing items often. If there is a real problem, have the child's hearing and speech evaluated by a pediatrician. For occasional biting, try these suggestions:

☐ React quickly and clearly, by saying something such as "No! Never bite people!" Warn your child what will happen if she bites again. (See "Methods of Discipline, pages 14–16.)

☐ Biting can occur when your child is overwhelmed with an emotion, including love. When you see a bite coming, quickly say "Kiss Mommy!" This may take a couple of weeks of reminding, but at least it's a positive response.

☐ Ask yourself if anything has changed recently in your child's life. Is he going to a new play group? Maybe the kids are older and he's having a hard time dealing with them. Have you taken away the bottle or pacifier? Maybe he needs it back.

☐ If biting occurs in a frustrating situation, avoid the situation until your child can deal with it.

☐ Your child may be feeling powerless. Boost her self-esteem by letting her make some decisions for herself.

☐ If your child bites when he is angry, show him other ways to express his anger. He could punch his pillow or run around the dining-room table.

☐ Reward your child each time he expresses his anger verbally instead of biting.

☐ Human bites are serious. If your child has been bitten, cleanse the area thoroughly, even if the skin does not appear to have been broken. (See page 221.)

☐ If another child is biting your child, do *not* pull them apart. Instead, pinch the nostrils of the biter so she will have to release her grip to breathe.

THE BOTTLE/THE PACIFIER/THE THUMB

When you are trying to change a habit, keep in mind that the child should be ready to do it; otherwise it's a losing battle. For instance, if the child is down to one or two bottles a day or sucks the pacifier only at night, he'll probably be willing to give it up.

There is no medical evidence that any of these habits are harmful to a toddler, with one exception: To prevent tooth decay, a child should never have a bottle in bed at night unless it's filled only with water. Most parents just don't like the sight of a two-year-old always sucking on something. Remember, though, that these habits fill a need. They comfort the child and serve as an outlet for tension and anxiety. Extra love and attention will help your child make the transition.

☐ Get the habit down to once a day before you try to end it.

☐ Try to change only one habit or undesirable behavior at a time. Praise works wonders, as do plenty of hugs and kisses.

☐ Try cutting a small hole in the pacifier or otherwise altering its shape.

☐ Dip the pacifier in pickle juice (or anything that's unpleasant but not harmful).

☐ *"We conveniently forgot her pacifiers at a favorite aunt's house and we [her father and mother] carried on and on about 'How could we have forgotten, etc., etc.' She found that most amusing, and it gave her an opportunity to demonstrate what a big girl she was."*

☐ Hide the pacifier and pretend it's lost. Get your toddler to join in the search for it. Find it every day for about three days. On the fourth day, you and your toddler will not have any luck finding it.

☐ Ready to take your child off the bottle? Try juice boxes. Stick the straw into the child's mouth and give a little squeeze right away. Usually this starts the sucking action, and the child carries on.

☐ Tell him the doctor says he can only have one bottle a day and he must drink it sitting up.

☐ Very gradually mix more and more water into the milk or juice your child loves in her bottle. She'll discover that liquids taste better from a cup.

☐ Take advantage of any change of locale—a vacation, for

instance. Just before you go home, encourage your child to drop his bottles into the wastebasket by saying "We don't have room for these bottles in our suitcases if we're going to take (name a special toy or book) back with us."

☐ *"I bought my daughter a baby doll and told her that when she was ready to give up her own bottle, she would also be ready to be a mommy to this doll. I was very firm—if she wasn't ready to give up the bottle she could not play with the new doll, and after a week or two of indecision, I was rewarded with success!"*

☐ Buy a special cup with her name on it (or with her favorite cartoon character) and explain that she may use it when she no longer needs the bottle. One parent's technique was even more elaborate: *"One day some very nice people came by when we were, unfortunately, out and took her bottles which they needed for a new baby. They left her a special gift: a beautiful silver grown-up cup!"* Make sure the people (or animals, whatever) are of the *very nice* variety so this technique doesn't create other problems, such as nightmares.

☐ Remember: No child has ever gotten on the school bus with a bottle or a pacifier in his mouth.

☐ Thumb-sucking will probably diminish when the child goes to nursery school and either encounters peer pressure or finds other ways to amuse himself.

☐ Nothing you can do will prevent thumb-sucking until the child is ready to give it up. Punishment and any harsh measures (taping the thumb, etc.) will just increase resistance and anxiety. You can, however, request that sucking take place only at home or in the child's room. Usually he'll go along with this.

Fascinations

Your two- or three-year-old is wonderfully curious and will most likely be fascinated by and will ask questions about the following:

☐ Genitals: his, hers and yours. Some typical questions— A girl: "Where is my penis?" A boy: "Why does my penis get big (or hard)?" "Where is Mommy's penis?" One mother who traveled with her child on public transportation reports being very happy (no matter what the experts say) that her child called everything by a baby name so no one else knew what she was talking about.

When one father was waiting in line at McDonald's, his daughter turned around, punched him in the crotch and announced, "Daddy, there's your penis!"

☐ Excrement: his, hers, yours and the dog's. Playing with it is not uncommon.

☐ Birth and babies: "Does the baby in your tummy cry and want a bottle?" "Where was I before I was born?" A boy: "Why can't I get pregnant?"

☐ Death: "After you die, do you become a ghost?" "Do dead people fly?"

☐ Religion: "What does God look like?" "Do angels wear slippers?"

☐ Mythical beings, such as Santa Claus, the sandman, the Easter Bunny.

☐ Handicaps of any kind: "Why are his eyes funny?" "Why is that lady in a chair with wheels?"

Children's questions often seem direct but are frequently asked for reasons that are not easily apparent. It's a good idea to respond with something such as "What made you think of that?" or "What do you think?" (This will also buy you a little time to think of answers.) Frequently you'll get a response that shows you what your child is *really* asking, which is often easier to answer. For example, the question "Why is the sky blue?" might not need a scientific answer; the child might be wondering about the colors in heaven.

Once you've determined what the child wants to know, a short, honest, simple answer (and they're not always easy to come by) is best.

2
Relationships

The Toddler and the New Baby

BEFORE BIRTH

☐ Take your toddler along on your ob/gyn visits so she can hear the fetal heartbeat. *"My child took great pleasure in telling her friends that her baby says 'Beep, beep, beep.'"*

☐ Let the older child open the baby gifts that come in before and after birth and play with them, assuring him that the baby wants to share them.

☐ During pregnancy, help your toddler make a gift for the baby, such as a drawing for baby's room. Have it framed and gift-wrapped. Your toddler will feel so proud to give the baby his very own creation.

☐ Before the baby is born, establish a "quiet time" with your older children in the morning and/or the afternoon so that they can get used to it before the baby arrives and needs some peace for his naptime.

☐ Put a doll in the bassinet a couple of months before the baby comes. Show your child what you will do with the new baby and encourage her to help. The doll may become a member of the family, too!

THE NEW ARRIVAL

☐ Good advice from many parents: Have the baby "give" gifts to the older sibling(s). This can start right in the hospital if they are allowed to visit. One mother hid presents in a drawer and let the older children find them.

☐ Involve the older child in the baby's life right from the beginning. Have him select the homecoming outfit, ask him to help strap baby into the car seat on the way home from the hospital and the like.

☐ If your children haven't visited you in the hospital and are waiting at home for your arrival, they will be most anxious to see and hug you. When you get home, have your husband manage the baby while you greet your other children with open arms.

☐ When the toddler is allowed to hold the baby right away, it helps establish a loving bond between siblings. If you're worried about your child dropping the infant, have her hold the baby while she sits on the floor. No danger there, and what a difference when you're not worried and she's not worried.

☐ When baby comes home give the older child a new doll as his own baby. Don't be surprised if it gets some pretty rough treatment.

☐ Foster the "proud parent" in a toddler by letting *her* introduce the new baby to visitors.

☐ Have gifts ready in case guests don't bring any for the "new big brother/sister." And don't hesitate to take guests aside to remind them to fuss over the older sibling, too.

☐ Always refer to the new little one as "our" baby.

☐ Don't be surprised if your other child is very cool to the new baby. Imagine how you would feel if your husband brought home a new wife and tried to convince you what a good idea it was.

☐ Use the baby photos of your toddler to show him what he was like as a baby and to reassure him that he also had special parties in his honor, that friends brought *him* presents and so on.

☐ Ask the older child to teach the baby to smile, which will encourage smiling at every opportunity. When the baby finally smiles back, she will be thrilled. Praise her for teaching the baby something so important. (The mother who gave me this tip reports that her older child still teaches the baby things such as "how to do a puzzle or make her bed or clean up—my favorite.")

☐ As your older child watches you care for the baby, tell him that you want him to learn what you did for him when he was a newborn. Ask him to pretend he's the baby, and he will see how much you loved and cared for him.

☐ Keep a step stool next to the changing table so that little ones can watch and help. Or change the baby's diapers on the floor so that it's easy for your toddler to participate and ask questions.

☐ A special, exclusive job such as selecting the "right" diaper can help a toddler feel important. Be sure he knows he is the best one for the job, and praise him often for being such a good helper.

☐ It's much easier to like someone who likes *you*, so make sure your toddler knows the baby likes him.

☐ Be sure to explain to older children that the new baby can't do much yet. Toddlers often interpret an infant's lack of speech and playfulness as hostility.

☐ For the first few weeks that the baby is home, arrange for family members to take your toddler out to special places so she isn't just overwhelmed by the new baby.

☐ Explain to your toddler exactly how hard it is to take care of a baby and why the baby requires so much time and attention. Many parents forget that siblings often don't understand *why* a baby has to eat and get changed so frequently. And it doesn't hurt to complain a bit to the older child about all the time a baby takes up and repeat how lucky you are to have a big boy/girl who is such a help.

☐ If you're breast-feeding, express your milk into a bottle occasionally and let your toddler feed the baby.

☐ Let the toddler sit on your lap while you're nursing or bottle-feeding. There's plenty of room for two. Tell stories or read to the toddler.

☐ Be sure to give your child a bottle for feeding his doll while you're feeding the baby. One breast-feeding mother reported that her son used a rubber band to attach two bottles together so he could switch from one to the other, just like Mommy.

☐ Now and then let your toddler stay on your lap while the *baby* waits.

☐ Set limits for the baby as well as for the toddler. Make sure that big brother or sister has special time alone with you as well as special toys that are not for the baby to play with.

☐ Encourage your child to work off her frustrations on a punching bag. Ideally she will hit it rather than the baby.

☐ When an older child picks on a younger, don't reward the older one even with scolding. Instead, lavish attention on the younger child and when everyone is happy, explain to the older that when she's nice, she'll get attention.

☐ Emphasize the older child's "seniority" by giving her new privileges: sleeping in a larger bed, a new place at the dinner table, the responsibility of setting the table, use of the telephone (with help) or an advanced toy.

☐ Tell your toddler to let you know whenever she needs a little extra loving.

☐ A stroller for twins is great for an infant and toddler.

☐ A baby gate or a latching screen door on the baby's doorway will keep toddlers and animals out when baby is napping, and you'll still be able to hear her. Or, close her door, and use an inexpensive baby monitor to listen for her.

☐ Cover your baby's playpen with mosquito netting to catch all the trucks and other toys that your toddler may dump on top of the baby. You can buy these playpen nets at any store that sells baby furniture. Never leave the baby unattended with the netting.

☐ Keep a supply of special but useful things (fancy socks or underwear, books, puppet gloves) wrapped up and hidden away. When you've really got a jealousy problem and nothing is working, use one of these items to distract your toddler. It is surprising how a little surprise can ease the tension enormously.

☐ Check your library or bookstore for books you can read to your child about the arrival of a new baby.

Learning to Share

Teaching a two to share is an uphill struggle. It takes many months and many contacts with other children before sharing is finally done willingly. Don't breathe that sigh of relief when it does happen, though; it's a beginning, but there will be backsliding again and again well into the threes.

☐ To give yourself some perspective on sharing, ask yourself if you would be happy about sharing *your* treasures— your china or crystal or car.

☐ Use the word "borrow" instead of "share." If you have borrowed books and toys from the library, your child understands that borrowed things are *returned,* and this concept will make sharing easier.

☐ Emphasize early on all the things you and he share— cooking tools and coloring books, for example. Quite often the first time the word (and concept of) sharing comes up is when your child snatches his toy away from a little friend. Learning to share will be easier to master if sharing is practiced in less traumatic situations.

☐ When you ask "Do you want to share your toy?" you're setting yourself up for a negative answer. Asking *which* toy she would like to share will be much more successful.

☐ Praise sharing lavishly when it happens; if it goes unacknowledged and unrewarded, it won't be repeated willingly. And do make sure that sharing is reciprocated.

☐ Friends who visit can be asked to bring a few toys of their own so your child doesn't feel she has to give up everything.

☐ In a play group have each child bring one of his own toys to the other child's house.

☐ If one won't share, give the other something highly desirable, and sharing will start quickly!

☐ Collect a box of toys that don't belong to anyone in particular and are just for sharing. Tag or rummage sales are good places to look for inexpensive toys to fill the box.

☐ Keep a box of toys that comes out only when guests visit. These toys will be new to your child, so he probably won't mind sharing his "old" toys.

☐ It is much easier for children to share when they are offered something in exchange. Teach children to offer a trade when they want to play with someone else's toy.

☐ Let the child rather than the adult decide when he is through with a toy. You may be surprised how quickly a child will share if he is allowed to finish playing with the toy. Remind other children that the child using the toy will want it back if he has not finished with it.

☐ Don't always produce a second toy whenever there is a problem. Children will learn to share only by being in situations in which they *have* to share.

☐ Tell the child she can put a special toy or two away if she just cannot share it. Surprisingly enough, this makes sharing the rest of the toys much easier. Do the choosing and putting away before the playmate arrives.

☐ Either have two riding toys (preferably the same) or put yours away before you have visitors in order to avoid inevitable battles.

☐ If your child won't share a toy because it's her "favorite," ask her what her next favorite toy is and then time the sharing. The friend plays with favorite #2 first for 10 minutes, then they switch.

☐ Use a kitchen timer to time turns. Children don't resent it; it's a neutral referee.

☐ An egg timer works well, too, and children like watching the sand.

☐ An alternative: Look at your watch and go "bong" at the appropriate moment.

☐ Let the child who is waiting hold a watch with a second hand and do the timing.

☐ When children just can't share a toy, remove it. This will cause *great* howls of rage from both children, but after using this technique a couple of times, all you will then have to do is remind them what will happen if they don't share.

Sharing Within the Family

☐ Remind your toddler often that sharing with a baby is easy. If an object is shared without fussing, the baby will tire of it quickly, drop it and go on to something else.

☐ An indoor seesaw really teaches siblings to cooperate.

☐ An old trick: If there is any dispute about the last piece of dessert, have one child (the oldest, usually) cut it in half, but let the other child choose the piece he wants first. You will find the division is exactly equal.

☐ Teach siblings to share by making a game of it. Cut out pictures of toys or just use cut-out shapes. Give children a few pictures to "play" with. Then let them practice sharing.

☐ From a mother of triplets: *"The magic words are 'When you're ready.' They work 95 percent of the time. For example, Becky wants the toy Casey has, and they're both screaming 'Mine!' I'll tell Becky to tell Casey 'I'm next.' Then I ask Casey to give the toy to Becky 'when you're ready.' Casey responds with 'No, mine!' and I say, 'I know it's yours. You don't have to give it up now, just when you're ready.' Casey nods with great satisfaction, hugs the toy, then gives it to Becky. Of course, Casey loves the praise she gets in response."*

☐ Sometimes sharing is achieved peacefully when you ask an older child to show a younger sibling how a certain toy works or what you do with it.

☐ If an older sibling can't share her toys with her baby brother, don't allow her to play with *any* of his toys. A few days of this will teach the meaning of sharing.

☐ If it's difficult for your toddler to share you with the rest of your family, set aside specific times that are *his* and his alone for playing, not doing chores, errands or cleanup. One mother reported, *"Thursday morning (after all the other kids are in school) is my exclusive time with my daughter. She can choose to do anything she wants with me. Having that time to look forward to and talk about makes the week a little easier."*

Manners

☐ Good manners will help a child feel good about himself. Treat your child with courtesy and consideration, and he will learn to treat others the same way.

☐ *"When our daughter doesn't say 'please,' we tell her, 'I can't hear you when you ask like that.' She learned quickly, and now it's a habit."*

☐ *"To teach manners at the table, we use a signal system. One finger is put up in the air when anyone sees anyone else talking with their mouth full. The child (or adult) is reminded good-naturedly without constant verbal nagging."*

☐ Good manners at dinner rate an after-dinner mint.

☐ Remind your child that you will not do what he wants until you hear "may I" and "please."

3

Toilet Training

Here's what was said over and over about toilet training:

☐ Wait until the child is ready. If you push or insist, you'll be engaged in a battle you can't win.

☐ Don't set some arbitrary time by which you feel your child should be trained. There is no set age that is "right" for training.

☐ Don't let *anyone* push you into it. The pressure from friends and relatives can be enormous. Be strong.

☐ When the child is ready, training is rapid and always successful.

How do you know the child is ready? Here are some signs:

☐ Imitating parental behavior.

☐ Understanding and obeying directions without undue resistance.

☐ Finding more pleasure in pleasing you than in being negative.

☐ Desiring to put things away; being orderly.

☐ Being aware of elimination activity and telling you when it occurs.

☐ Feeling that wet or dirty diapers are unpleasant.

☐ Staying dry for several hours or overnight.

☐ Verbally expressing the desire for big-girl underwear, no diapers and the like.

Before Training Begins

☐ Make *sure* your child understands the vocabulary you will use during the training process. For instance, many children of this age do not really understand the difference between "before" and "after." This becomes crucial when you're asking the child to tell you *before* he wets.

☐ In warm weather, if you can, let the child run around outside without any pants. Going without pants will cause more awareness of urination when it occurs, and she may start telling you after it happens (or even before, if you're lucky).

☐ Often the greatest incentive for children to begin training is the prospect of wearing fancy underwear instead of diapers. When you feel your child is physically ready, begin to point out that neighbor Jimmy wears Superman underwear because he goes to the toilet by himself or that cousin Kate can wear frilly underpants because she doesn't get them wet.

☐ Buying a potty chair early and having it available may prompt interest in its use. Put it in the bathroom and wait for the child to ask about it.

☐ Encourage your child to sit on the potty (with clothes on) while you're on the toilet. It gets children used to it.

☐ Try switching from comfortable disposables to cloth diapers. Unlike disposables, cloth gets cold and feels wet. The discomfort may be enough to motivate your child to try the toilet.

☐ Slightly older children are terrific role models. Trained three-, four- and five-year-olds are usually very proud of their accomplishments and if invited to will not mind in the least showing your child how they use the toilet. This often inspires little ones far more than hearing how Mommy and Daddy use the toilet.

☐ Check your library or bookstore for books you can read to your child about toilet training.

The Potty

The potty chair, pro and con:

PRO:

☐ It's portable and can be used where the child is most comfortable (in front of the TV, in the kitchen with Mom).

☐ The child's feet can touch the ground.

☐ There is no implied danger of falling in.

☐ It is the child's own, special seat.

CON:

☐ The child will have to be retrained to a toilet.

☐ Some children who are used to a potty will not go in a

regular toilet, which makes for great difficulties when you're away from home.

☐ Some children refuse to use them because they want to use the toilet like an adult.

There are also seats that snap onto the adult toilet seat, which solve some problems. It is probably best to have a potty on hand during the training period. Your child will choose her own favorite method and, while she's learning, go with what she prefers.

☐ Do not buy a potty with a detachable bowl that's hard for the child to take out and empty by himself. Test this before you buy.

☐ Fancy toilet seats with goose heads (or whatever) in the front are very difficult for the child to use. Usually a parent has to lift the child on or off.

☐ Take off the guards on potty seats. If a child gets hurt by one, it can slow down toilet training. Boys can easily be taught to hold their penis down while they urinate.

☐ If you use a potty chair, a foldable one (some even turn into footstools) is practical, especially for families who travel a great deal by automobile.

☐ If your child is afraid of the noise the urine or BM makes hitting the water, a potty chair makes sense.

The Teaching Process

☐ First discuss using the toilet with your child and watch for a spark of interest. If it comes, start. If you get a flat "no," forget it for a while. Bring the subject up casually every so often, and take your cue from the child.

☐ Start giving the child *lots* of liquids. Put him on the potty after meals and before bedtime. These are the times when you're most likely to catch something. If your child is agreeable, put him on more often.

Make sitting fun by reading or singing. Once he eliminates, praise him highly. He'll soon get the idea that it's *good* to void on the potty, and you're on your way.

☐ Some children refuse to be put on the potty at all. For such a child to be trained, she must be able to sense her body's signals and get herself to the toilet. Take her diapers off and don't put any pants on. (Obviously summertime is best for this.) Keep her in the kitchen if you have to and stick close to her. Have a potty close by and try to get her on it when she begins.

☐ Teach a doll or teddy bear first while your child watches. Once the procedure is carefully explained and understood, involve your child by having him teach the doll what to do.

☐ It helps to use a doll that wets to show the child what he is supposed to do.

☐ Don't bother to toilet train late in your pregnancy. Regression is so common when a new sibling appears, and toilet habits are the first to go. Wait a few months till things have settled down.

☐ Make sure when you begin that you can *really* devote about a week to the child. Free yourself from all commitments. You've got to *be* there, ready to spring, encourage, praise and calmly mop up messes all day long. You will be *rewarded* by a well-trained, happy child. But if you try to squeeze training in and around other engagements, it may not go so well. (Note: Your child may not be fully trained in a week but will be well on the way so that your schedule can be resumed.)

☐ Wait till summer to start, if possible. There are less clothes to deal with, and you can even let the child run around without clothes, which makes getting to the potty on time easier. Also, accidents outdoors are easier to deal with.

☐ A child's summertime question: "If it's okay to go around in a wet bathing suit, why isn't it okay to have wet pants?" Better have an answer ready. The mother whose logical daughter asked this question reported that a perpetually wet suit did her in, and the child remained untrained until the fall.

☐ Use a squirt bottle (such as the peri bottle you had in the hospital after you gave birth) to teach your child about urination.

☐ Make sure the child wears pants and underpants that are *easy* to slip on and off by herself. Put the overalls away.

☐ If you want your child to wear overalls during toilet training, sew Velcro fasteners onto the straps.

☐ Consider using disposable training pants during early training. This makes accidents easier to ignore. When accidents slow and/or stop, go on to regular training pants.

☐ Once your child shows an active interest in toilet training, clear out the diapers. Using training pants 24 hours a day necessitates a lot of laundry for a short time, but the child's "big" image pays off. As one mother commented, *"My son had diarrhea right after we started training, and since it was impossible for him to control it, we put rubber pants on top of the underpants and he felt much better. He would have* hated *going back to diapers, and I think it would have been very confusing."*

☐ Use the thickest training pants you can find. *Every* child has accidents during toilet training; that's the way they learn. One mother reports: *"I have mixed feelings about fancy training pants. I started training at about 31 months, and as it was touch-and-go at first, I bought two pairs of little pants with blue and red airplanes on them. These instantly became his favorites and all he wanted to wear. And of course they got wet and/or soiled and had to be hand washed. They were an enormous nuisance. On the other hand, he was proud of them and enthusiastic about wearing them. I guess the moral of this story is: Buy plenty of the pants that become favorites, to save yourself some work."* (Note: This is not a bad investment, as good-quality underpants last a *long* time and will fit for years.)

☐ If your child has graduated to training pants but still has accidents, just lay a small (infant) diaper inside to catch anything. Or use diaper liners or disposable training pants.

☐ Set a timer to remind your child of potty time.

☐ To get your child to relax while on the toilet, sing, read to him or blow bubbles.

☐ *"During the training process, I let my daughter take the potty around to wherever she was comfortable. She relaxed more while watching TV or being where I was. Now she likes to have privacy in the bathroom, but in the beginning it helped her to be comfortable."*

☐ If your child is just toilet trained, buy a big pocketbook and one of those cup-type potties. Children always have to go in the most inconvenient places! They are great to keep in the car, too.

☐ Get used to the fact that once training begins, you will visit bathrooms wherever you shop. Remember, every store has to have a bathroom, even if the store owners don't want you to use it. If they give you any trouble (and some clerks do), explain sweetly that it's either the toilet or their floor. This gets quick action.

☐ Don't let your child get rigid about where he voids. Get him accustomed to a variety of places—including outdoors.

☐ Keep in mind that some children really like privacy when they use a portable potty. If you're encountering resistance when using the potty outside the home (or even inside), this may be the reason.

☐ Teach your child to sit backward on the toilet, holding onto the tank for support. Provide a small stool so toddlers can climb on easily. They feel very secure in this position (and love to see the "bubbles" they're making). It also eliminates the need for a special training seat, which helps when you're away from home.

☐ Boys want to imitate their fathers, so why make them sit down to urinate? Have a stool ready to use by the toilet so they can stand like a grown-up.

☐ Boys sometimes need to improve their aim. Float a square of toilet paper in the bowl as a target, or sprinkle confetti on the water for him to sink.

☐ Some children like to sit on the potty with a book. Many enjoy looking at toy catalogs, too.

☐ If your child really resists sitting on the toilet, she may be fearful of something. Some children worry about being bitten by sharks or fish in the toilet. In the most casual, gentle way, try to see if this might be the case. Airing these fears may help overcome them.

☐ Remember, some kids don't like to see their waste disappear down the toilet. Many feel it is part of them. Also, children can be confused when adults make a big fuss over a BM and then flush it away.

☐ Some children are frightened by the noise of the toilet flushing. If it seems to be a problem, flush after the child leaves the bathroom.

☐ If a child really resists, he's not ready yet. Put training off for a few weeks or months. *It is not worth a battle, and anyway you won't win!*

Regression

If a child who has been dry for quite a while begins to wet again (and it's common), there is probably a specific reason for it. Is there a new sibling at home? Extra tension? A move or change of locale? Your child needs your support at this time more than ever. Some suggestions:

☐ Try to pinpoint and alleviate the cause of the regression.

☐ Assure the child that this state is only temporary and he'll stop having accidents very soon.

☐ Devote extra time to the child.

☐ Keep your cool and don't punish. Your child needs support, not blame.

☐ Take off the pretty underwear and go back to diapers. Often this will motivate the child to be dry very quickly.

Rewards

We all praise our children as they begin to show progress in the toilet-training process. For some children the verbal praise and obvious delight of their parents is enough to motivate them to master new skills and retain what they've learned. But some children need more. Here are some ideas that parents have found successful:

☐ The star reward system:

- Buy stars to glue or stick on a chart for each successful elimination. Let the child do it. Or let the child draw her own star on a giant calendar.
- Make sure everyone in the household sees and admires the star chart every day.
- Sometimes stars are enough. For more oomph, try totaling them to earn other rewards: 10 stars means lunch out or 20 stars means a trip to the park with Mom or Dad.

☐ Food rewards—cookies, candy, pretzels, gum—have all been used successfully, especially if they're not usually allowed.

• Make food rewards small (tiny candies) or your child just may not crave them after a while.
• When toileting has become a habit and accidents occur only now and then, taper off on these food rewards this way:

> Start to "forget" them. Involve your child in something fun while he's on the toilet and continue it afterward so he'll forget the reward. Or plan something very exciting for him to do the minute he gets off the toilet.
> Show him the cookie box (or whatever). Casually mention that when the last cookie is gone, there won't be any more. (This works only if your child doesn't understand you can buy more. Best not to let your child see you purchase his reward.)

☐ Keep a piggy bank in the bathroom and deposit a penny or a nickel for every deposit of hers!

☐ A girl might enjoy a barrette in her hair as a reward. Twenty barrettes may look silly to you, but your child may think it's great.

☐ Some children like to get stickers or ink stamps on their hands when they have success.

☐ For a child who really needs incentive, try this: gift-wrap a bunch of inexpensive toys, such as crayons or balloons, and leave them where he can see them to pique his curiosity—and greed. The thrill of getting a "present" for using the toilet will sometimes do the trick.

☐ Unhappy because she felt she was bribing her child with cookies, one mother felt much better when a friend suggested she think of the cookies as "positive reinforcement" rather than bribes.

☐ Remember: Rewards won't work if the child is not ready.

Personal Experiences

☐ From a mother of six: *"Each child trained at a different time, some at two years three months and one as early as 18 months. It really depends on the maturity of the child. When they seem ready, I work with them about a month before I begin the one week of potty training. I start to show displeasure at having to change a diaper ('Oh, no, not again!'—jokingly, of course). I instruct them to bring me a diaper when they 'mess' so they can be changed. Once they show that they are conscious of their movements by automatically bringing me a diaper, we start the intensified potty training.*

"I clear my calendar for a week so I can be with the child at all times. I feel if you start training and then put a diaper on the child because you have to go shopping or something, it just confuses them and they regress. So off goes the diaper, and about 20 minutes after drinking something, I take the child in to sit on the potty and we read books for about 5 minutes. If nothing happens, we leave the bathroom and try again about 10 minutes later. Eventually we catch something by accident and then do we make a big deal out of it! (My husband can always tell when we've started training because everyone's in the bathroom clapping and there are balloons everywhere!)

"We always stress the positive and get very excited by

success. Accidents are handled very casually with no blaming or fuss. After about a week of this, the child has gotten the hang of it and doesn't even want diapers anymore. Sometimes they train day and night at the same time."

☐ *"At two years, my son urinated in the toilet, but saved his BMs for the diaper at naptime. Finally, after a year of this, we said, 'That's it—no more diapers ever.' He never wet the bed, and after about seven BMs in his pants, he went on the potty. It was as if he had invented his own waste disposal machine, he was so ecstatic."*

☐ *"My son finally achieved bladder control with the help of Joey, a male doll that wet, but none of the conventional or even nonconventional methods worked for bowel control. So I tried an idea of my own: I decided to train Joey and let my son watch. I put Joey on the potty seat and we left him alone to have his BM. While my son was outside, I slipped into the bathroom and placed torn-up pieces of dark-brown construction paper in the toilet. Then I called my son in to check Joey's progress on the toilet, and he was amazed that Joey had made a BM in the toilet. Well, as outlandish as it may sound, he was so impressed that within 10 days of watching Joey have BMs, he was not only asking to sit on the potty but was also having bowel movements himself in the toilet instead of in his diaper."*

☐ *"I wanted to send my son to a nursery school that required that the children be toilet trained. So I started to train him at two and a half. He resisted, but I persisted, and we wound up having a year-long battle that is having its repercussions to this day.*

"By the time he was three and a half, I was so desperate that I called Dr. Ames at the Gesell Institute. She told me

to relax and to tell him *that at four he'd be able to use the toilet and not to worry anymore about it (the power of positive thinking). At about the same time we were starting to go to a pool where he was not allowed in with diapers. He wanted to go in that pool very badly. Who knows what did the trick, but within a few weeks he was trained.*

"*If there is one piece of advice in your book you should emphasize, capitalize and red-letter, it is this about toilet training:* Relax and cool it."

(Note: If the nursery school requires that all children be trained and yours is not ready, look for another school or wait till next year to send her. A sensitive teacher will often work with you if your child is having difficulties. If the school is rigid about this, is it worth it?)

☐ "*My first child was two plus, still in diapers, on the bottle, and I was frantic. A friend whose opinion I respected gave me the best advice:* 'Don't worry,' *she said, and added,* 'There's never been a child yet who has gotten on that kindergarten bus with either a diaper or a bottle!' *That seemed to put the entire situation in proper perspective for me, and the more I relaxed, the more interested my daughter became in giving up her diapers and bottle!*"

Bed-wetting

Bed-wetting is normal. Some children have a few accidents and then learn to stay dry, but for many children, nighttime control is very difficult. Certainly punishment, anger or derision will only make the problem worse. After all, the child is not consciously in control while sleeping, and some children sleep so deeply they just don't receive their body's signals. Patience, understanding and the following suggestions may help. And do reassure your child that he *will* learn to stay dry at night.

☐ If bed-wetting starts suddenly, for no apparent reason, it might be due to a bladder infection or another physical ailment. Check with your doctor.

☐ Leave diapers on as long as you possibly can. Changing a diaper in the morning is *much* easier than changing wet sheets and pajamas in the middle of the night. One mother reports, *"At three and a half, the overnight diaper was driving my son crazy. (He said the plastic 'stuck' to him.) I should have switched to cloth diapers and plastic pants, but instead we encouraged him to sleep without the diaper. (He had never woken up with a dry diaper, and I ought to have known he wasn't ready to stay dry through the night.) Well, we've had a year now of training, and I'd say he's wet the bed, off and on, for about half of it. And when he does wet, he usually wakes me to change his wet pajamas. Who needs this?"*

☐ Let the child sleep without any pants or pajama bottoms so that she won't forget and think she has diapers on.

☐ Blanket sleepers are impractical for children learning to stay dry. They're hard for the child to unzip in the middle of the night, and they're very unpleasant and cold when soaked.

☐ Take your child to the bathroom to urinate before you go to bed.

☐ Keep a potty or a cup by the bed in case your child has to urinate in the middle of the night. That long trek to the bathroom may just be too much for a sleepy child. Leave a night-light on so he'll be able to see.

☐ Cut out all drinks two hours before bedtime.

☐ Colds sometimes cause bed-wetting.

☐ Some children react to being cold in bed by wetting.

☐ Sometimes a concrete, visual reminder/reward helps. Right before bedtime put a shiny penny (or something) on his bedside table, with the promise that he may put it in his piggy bank if he stays dry. This seems to work better than just the promise of getting a penny in the morning.

☐ Let your child choose some new decorative sheets. This may give her an incentive to keep them dry.

☐ Have the child sleep on a flannel-covered rubber pad. Then, if it gets wet, you or your child can just take it off and the bed will be dry.

☐ You and your child may find it helpful to discuss the problem with your pediatrician. Says one parent, *"My son's bed-wetting coincided exactly with his first month in nursery school; up till then he'd been pretty dry. Our pediatrician, after checking to make sure there was no physical reason for the bed-wetting, just said casually (but emphatically), 'Don't worry about it. It will soon stop.' And, by golly, it did."*

(Note: You may wish to call your pediatrician before you take the child in to find out what advice he/she will give. But a positive statement from a "higher authority" may be all the child needs.)

General Observations

☐ A word of comfort: when children train late, they train well.

☐ Some schools base their intellectual development records on the age a child was toilet trained and will ask you when it was. If you think this is none of their business, just write "Don't know."

☐ You will hear many wonderful and funny observations from your child during this period, such as this one from a little girl who said, "Mommy, did you know Daddy tinkles with a hose?" Do keep a record of them.

Safety and Health

Accidents at home and in cars are the leading cause of death among one- to five-year-olds. As Dr. Rose Ames, a pediatrician for 30 years, puts it, "The best prevention is always having the child in sight or knowing exactly where the child is and what he is doing. Always listen if the child is not in sight. If you can't figure out what is going on, go and see for yourself. This is usually the time when the child ingests drugs or other poisonous substances that have not been put away." Most parents learn that when there's silence, there's trouble. So keep an eye on your child, and use these tips to make his environment as safe as possible.

General Home Safety

☐ You may have to rechildproof your house for a very curious and mobile two-year-old and move valuable and/or dangerous belongings even higher.

☐ Keep outside doors *locked*. You can't always be sure that children will stay put during naptime or any other time, and they might wander out into the street.

☐ Attach chimes or bells to the door of your child's room and the outside doors so that you'll hear them open.

☐ Always listen for the patter of little feet going near dangerous areas, such as the bathroom or basement.

☐ Put an automatic door closer (the kind you see on screen doors) on the basement door or any door leading to stairs.

☐ Do not trust a gate to keep a toddler out of a backyard pool. Install an alarm in your house, and keep it on while you're inside. You will soon know if your child goes out a door or window.

☐ Place a mirror in strategic places in the kitchen (or elsewhere) so you can watch your children playing in other rooms.

☐ As soon as you can, teach your child his first and last name, his address and his phone number. If you sing it in a jingle-type tune, it will be easy to memorize.

☐ If you answer the door or the phone, take your child with you. In the time it takes to go to the door, toddlers can swallow poison or climb a bookcase and fall off.

☐ Forget safety locks, especially if you have other children around. Someone will forget to lock. Also, some toddlers are extremely adept at unlocking "childproof" latches. They consider it a challenge and are better at it than you are.

☐ Fill all empty electrical outlets in walls with blank plastic plugs.

☐ When traveling, take your own electric outlet covers. They're essential when visiting Grandma, too.

☐ Avoid products that come in aerosol cans. They are very tempting to play with and too easy to misuse.

☐ Keep all baby powder, foot powder, any powder, out of reach. Inhaling powder can be very dangerous.

☐ Screw bookcases to the wall. Why do toddlers love to climb bookcases? Because they're there.

☐ Plastic bags can suffocate children. Never allow them to be played with. Knot and pierce them, and dispose of them out of children's reach.

☐ Take off and dispose of all plastic bags from the cleaners at the shop so you won't even have them in the car with the child.

☐ If there are dry-cleaner bags in the home, pierce a hole and tie a knot in the bottom so the child won't be able to get his head in them.

☐ Pierce and tie knots in dry-cleaner bags before you throw them away so that they're not harmful if found.

☐ Children have drowned in buckets and ice coolers with small amounts of liquid in them. Always empty large containers of any liquid or ice.

☐ Call the Coalition for Container Safety at (800) 282-5385 for stickers to place on plastic buckets to warn of the drowning danger.

☐ Don't have glass furniture around toddlers, especially glass coffee tables. Children can fall through them and be cut severely.

☐ Put colored decals on glass doors at your child's eye level so she'll notice the glass.

☐ If glass or china breaks on the floor, be sure to wipe it well with a damp paper towel to remove all the tiny pieces that a broom can't pick up.

☐ Tape cardboard over any broken window and get it repaired immediately.

☐ Store empty glass bottles out of the reach of children.

☐ Don't keep anything in front of a window that a child can use to climb on.

☐ Windows should have screens, gates, locks or window guards. If they do not, open them from the top only.

☐ Put "tot-finder" decals on your child's window facing outside. These let firefighters know instantly which rooms might contain helpless children. You can usually get the decals free from your local fire department.

☐ Make sure you have a working smoke detector in each child's room as well as other locations recommended by your fire department.

☐ One family's routine: *"Our son is our fire inspector. Once a month he puts on his fireman's hat, and he and his dad go around the house to check smoke detectors, fire extinguishers and exits (to make sure they're clear). We practice the stop-drop-roll technique (the procedure to be followed if clothes catch on fire) after inspection. He loves to give us the order to stop, drop and roll; meanwhile he's learning a lifesaving technique."*

☐ Be sure all your phones have emergency telephone numbers (see form on page 231) taped to them for instant referral by you or anyone in your house. Your local

Poison Control Center probably has free preprinted stickers with their number available for the asking.

☐ Carpeting on your stairs is a good idea.

☐ Tie a rope under the banister so children will have something to hold on to when they're walking up and down.

☐ Light stairs well and keep them free of toys and clutter.

☐ Accordion stretch gates are not safe. Use the net kind instead. If you put the net gate at the top of the stairs, be sure it is attached *securely* to the walls. Also be aware that adventurous toddlers like to climb over gates. It may be unwise to gate the top of the stairs.

☐ Folding (bifold) doors can pinch little fingers unless they're carefully secured.

☐ Never let children run with anything sharp or pointy in their hands or mouths. Straws, sticks, pencils, Popsicle sticks, and the like are all potentially dangerous.

☐ To prevent children from locking themselves in rooms, remove all interior locks or be sure you have keys handy. Also keep a spare house key outside somewhere; mischievous children have been known to lock their parents out of the house!

☐ If certain inside doors must have locks, teach your children to unlock them. If they can lock, they can unlock; it just takes some practice.

☐ On grocery-shopping days, dress your toddler in overalls. When you put him into the seat of the cart, tie his shoulder straps in back of him to the back of the seat. Make sure his clothes can't get caught around his neck if he tries to move, though.

- [ ] Never ever take your eyes off a toddler in a supermarket cart, even if he is well secured.

In the Kitchen

- [ ] Turn all pot and pan handles toward the back of the stove so that a child can't grab them. Use the back burners as much as possible.

- [ ] Never put a hot beverage in a cup near the edge of a counter where a child could grab it.

- [ ] If your child can reach the control knobs on the stove, remove them when you're not using them. If you can't remove them, glue something repellent on them to remind the child not to touch. One mother used plastic bugs.

- [ ] *"Avoid those* thin *plastic training cups with strawlike tops. My child bit off and swallowed a piece of plastic from one."*

- [ ] Always check the oven/broiler before you turn it on to preheat if it's within a toddler's reach. *"My husband averted near disaster because he saw our two-year-old stick the newspaper in the oven."*

- [ ] Don't add electric dishwasher detergent to the cups in the door until you're ready to close the door and start the machine. When the door is open, it's just the right height for children to investigate, and that detergent is dangerous.

- [ ] When your tot is just learning to clear tables and help clean up, switch to unbreakable plates and glasses for a while.

☐ Store unused refrigerators and freezers with doors removed.

In the Bathroom

☐ Turn the water temperature down in your home so your child won't be accidentally scalded: 120°F or 52°C is safe.

☐ Never let your child play in the bathroom. Children have drowned in toilets and fractured their skulls from bathroom falls.

☐ Put some red paint or nail polish on the hot-water faucet in the tub or sink and teach your child *not* to turn it on. You could paint the cold-water faucet green and use the traffic-light analogy.

☐ Be sure the rubber mat in the bathtub covers the whole bottom, or cover it with rubber nonslip stickers.

☐ Don't leave bath mats on the floor in front of the tub. Toddlers can trip or skid on them and hit their heads on the tub. Even the rubber-backed mats are unsafe.

☐ Do not store medicines of any kind in the medicine chest or cabinet. In addition to the potential hazards, most medications become inactive when subjected to heat and/or moisture.

In the Car

☐ See pages 166–170 for information on car seats and related car safety.

☐ Never leave children alone in the car unsupervised. They

seem to know instinctively how to release the emergency brake.

☐ Be sure to keep the de-icer spray *locked* in the trunk. A small amount in the eyes can cause blindness.

☐ After you've put children into a car, have them put their hands on top of their heads. Then you'll know just where their fingers are when you shut the car door.

☐ If only one adult is present, don't allow children to eat in the car. If they gag or choke, you can't respond.

☐ Do not store medications in the glove compartment.

☐ When your toddler gets out of the car and must wait there for a few moments, ask her to *hold* the handle, *touch* the taillight or *stand* on the white line. This works better than "Stay there." Don't take your eyes off her in any case.

☐ If you have a car accident and must remove your child from the car before emergency medical help arrives, remove him *in* his safety seat in case of spinal cord damage.

Outdoors

☐ In the car or on a walk, train your child to watch the cars and traffic lights and tell *you* when it's safe to go.

☐ Check your yard for poisonous plants and plants with poisonous berries and remove them. (See list on pages 68–70.)

☐ Teach your child not to play either in front or in back of swings.

☐ Rigid swing seats are slippery and dangerous if they hit a child in the head. For your own swing set, purchase the flexible seat that hugs the body.

☐ If the swing seat is slippery, attach foam rubber to it with tape.

☐ Don't let your child swing on his stomach. It's too easy to twist and swing at an angle, and before you know it, the child on the next swing will hit him inadvertently.

☐ Be sure to use nylon, manila or other strong rope for swings. Clothesline rope should *not* be used, as it frays easily.

☐ A four- to six-inch layer of sand or bark mulch is a good foundation under playground equipment in case of falls. It also dries out quickly after a rain.

☐ Check playground equipment for exposed hardware that can scratch skin or rip clothes. Cover any you find with tape.

☐ Slides can be dangerous for very young children, who may choke if their clothing gets caught as they are sliding down. If you cannot watch them at all times, you may wish to remove the slide for a few years.

☐ If your child is playing in or near the driveway—*under your supervision, of course*—park your car at the end of the driveway to keep other vehicles from entering.

☐ To prevent your child from accidentally rolling into the street on any of his wheeled vehicles, place a ladder at the end of your driveway.

Pet Safety

Toddlers love animals, but their enthusiasm can be harmful to themselves and pets. Remember these guidelines:

☐ Do not let your child touch any animal before asking permission from you and the animal's owner.

☐ Teach your child to approach animals quietly and calmly with her arms down. No running, waving, jumping or yelling.

☐ When approaching a dog, slowly extend the hand palm down for the dog's inspection.

☐ Do not let your child put his face against an animal's face.

☐ Teach your child how to pat an animal gently.

☐ If you have an aging pet, watch for changes in temperament. Many wonderful cats and dogs become intolerant of children's "loving" as they age.

FOR MORE INFORMATION

☐ For special holiday safety tips, see pages 210–211.

☐ For toy safety tips, see pages 183–184.

☐ The U.S. Consumer Product Safety Commission has many free booklets. To receive a complete list, write Office of Information and Public Affairs, U.S. Consumer Products Safety Commission, Washington, D.C. 20207, or call (800) 638-CPSC from anywhere in the continental U.S. Pamphlets available for free include: "Electrical

Safety Room by Room Audit Checklist" (English and Spanish); "Handbook for Playground Safety, Volume I"; "General Guidelines, Children and Pool Safety Checklist"; and "Backyard Pool—CPSC Safety Alert."

☐ If you know of a product intended for use by children that seems unsafe to you, call the Consumer Product Safety Commission at the number above.

☐ Call the National Safety Council at (800) 621-7619 Ext. 1300 for a free catalog of their low-cost safety publications, such as "The E's of Electrical Safety" and "Playground Safety." You may also write to them at 444 N. Michigan Avenue, Chicago, IL 60611.

☐ For a list of helpful, inexpensive pamphlets about pets and pet care, send a self-addressed, stamped envelope to: American Humane Association, P.O. Box 3597, Englewood, CO 80155-3597, or call (800) 227-4645 for more information.

Poisons

☐ Keep all dangerous substances in their *original* containers.

☐ Always return poisonous products to their appropriate places immediately after use. Eighty percent of all poisonings occur when a product is in use, not in storage.

☐ Keep a bottle of ipecac syrup in your diaper bag and write the number of the Poison Control Center on the label. Call before administering it, as ipecac shouldn't be used for some poisons.

☐ Read all labels carefully and administer medicine exactly

according to directions. Always turn the light on at night to measure medication accurately.

☐ Never let your child see you take medication. Children love to imitate parents. If they do see you, explain the purpose of the medication but warn them not to touch it.

☐ Nonprescription medications are just as dangerous as prescription medications. Treat them with respect.

☐ Most children's medications, fluoride pills and vitamin pills are sweet like candy. Be sure to make it clear to your child that they are *not* candy. They can be harmful if taken in large quantities, so keep them out of reach.

☐ Never tell a child that medicines for him or for anyone in the family are vitamins. Children see cartoon shows in which the characters take a whole bottle for energy, and might be tempted to do the same.

☐ Keep track of how much medicine is in jars or containers. In case of accidental poisoning, you'll have a better idea of what the child took.

☐ More and more manufacturers are making medications and poisonous products available in child-resistant packages. Buy these whenever possible, but be aware that "child-resistant" does not mean "childproof." You still must be careful with them.

☐ Discard all leftover medication and poisonous products in a place children cannot reach.

☐ Do not store cleaning agents on the same shelves as food.

☐ Products that are intended for the same purpose (such as dishwashing detergents) often vary in their degree of poison content. When you have a choice, buy the safest, mildest product. Call your local Poison Control Center for information about products before purchasing them.

☐ Children usually have good associations with pleasantly scented products and will be more prone to eat and/or drink them. When you can, buy products that are not scented.

☐ Explain to children as early as possible, and in whatever manner is necessary, that poisons are harmful and that children should stay away from them.

☐ Clean all ashtrays immediately. Children will try to eat anything, even cigarette butts.

☐ Do you have jewelry made from seeds, beans or grasses? Keep it away from your child.

☐ Be aware of the meaning on product labels of the words "danger," "warning" and "caution." "Danger" represents the highest degree of hazard; "warning" indicates an intermediate degree of hazard; "caution" is the lowest degree of hazard. One father wrote: *"It is interesting to note that the word 'danger' appears on at least a half-dozen items in our kitchen cabinets. Most people don't know that some of the most dangerous chemicals in a laboratory fall into the same category—sulfuric acid, nitric acid, hydrofluoric acid, etc. I'm not sure that some of this stuff should be in our homes at all, but if it is, it should be stored safely on top shelves only, never under a kitchen sink."*

☐ If your child has swallowed a poisonous substance, don't waste time reading the instructions on the container.

They are not always the best or most up-to-date. Call the Poison Control Center immediately!

☐ A common label on dangerous chemicals and medicines has been the skull and crossbones. Unfortunately, some children's cereal manufacturers, fast-food chains and amusement parks have chosen this "pirate" symbol as a trademark. This symbol is gradually being replaced by other poison warning symbols, such as Mr. Yuk, that better indicate to children (and adults) the effects of the contents of a package.

☐ Lead poisoning is a leading health problem for children today. Infants and toddlers are at the greatest risk because they constantly put things in their mouths. The Centers for Disease Control recommends routine blood testing beginning at one year old, but testing can start at six months when lead exposure is suspected (when children are living in old houses with peeling paint and/or old lead water pipes).

☐ Here are some items that can be found in homes and should be kept out of children's reach:

acids/alkali
aerosols
alcoholic beverages
ammonia
ant poisons
antifreeze
antiseptics
aspirin
bathroom bowl cleaner

bleach
boric acid
bubble bath
cigarettes/cigars/pipe
    tobacco
cleaning fluids
cologne/perfume/
    aftershave lotion
copper and brass cleaners

corn and wart removers

detergents, especially automatic dishwasher detergents

drain cleaners

drugs (prescription and nonprescription)

fertilizers

furniture polish

garden chemicals

glue

hair dyes

insecticides (insect poisons)

iodine

iron supplements or pills with added iron

kerosene

model cement

mouthwash

nail polish

nail polish remover

narcotics

oven cleaner

paint

paint thinner

permanent-wave solution

pesticides (insect/animal poisons)

petroleum distillates

pine oil

plants

rodenticides (rat/mouse poisons)

rubbing alcohol

shampoo

shaving cream

silver polish

turpentine

typewriter-cleaning fluid

vanilla extract

vitamins

window-washing solvent

☐ The following plants are poisonous. Some cause minor irritations; others can cause severe reactions. Avoid them in your home or garden. If your child chews on or swallows any part of any plant, call the Poison Control Center immediately.

almond tree

aloe ("burn plant")

amaryllis (bulb)

angel's trumpet

apple tree

apricot tree

autumn crocus
azalea
balsam pear
baneberry
beach apples
belladonna lily
bittersweet
bleeding heart
bloodroot
buttercup
caladium
cashew
castor bean
cherry tree
chinaberry tree
Christmas pepper
Christmas rose
comfrey
cowage
cow's horn
cowslip
creeping spurge
crown of thorns
daffodil (bulb)
daphne
death camas
delphinium
dieffenbachia (dumbcane)
elderberry
elephant ear
English holly
English ivy

false hellebore
foxglove
ginko (berries)
glory lily
golden chain tree
holly
horse chestnuts
hyacinth (bulb)
hydrangea
iris (bulb)
jack-in-the-pulpit
Jerusalem cherry
jessamine
jimson weed
jonquil (bulb)
lady slipper
lantana
larkspur
lily of the valley
locust tree
lupine
mace (in quantity)
mayapple
milkweed
mistletoe
monkshood (root)
moonseed
morning glory
mountain laurel
mushrooms (many)
narcissus (bulb)
nettle

nicotiana
nightshade
nutmeg (in quantity)
oak tree (acorns)
oleander
peach tree
peyote
philodendron
poinsettia
poison hemlock
poison ivy
poison oak
poison sumac
pokeweed
potato (leaves)
pothos
primrose
privet
rhododendron

rhubarb (leaves)
rosary pea (seeds)
sandbox tree
sassafras
skunk cabbage
snakeroot
sneezeweed
snow-on-the-mountain
snowdrop (bulb)
spider lily
sweet pea (seed)
tapioca plant
tobacco
tomato (leaves)
Virginia creeper
water hemlock
wisteria (seeds)
yew

FOR MORE INFORMATION

☐ Call the National Safety Council at (800) 621-7619 Ext. 1300 for a free catalog of their low-cost safety publications, such as "Stop Lead Poisoning" (in English and Spanish) and "Preventing Accidental Poisonings." This latter booklet includes cleaning-product tips, medication guidelines, and information about children and medications and household chemicals, and a quick response chart. You may also write to the National Safety Council at 444 N. Michigan Avenue, Chicago, IL 60611.

☐ For the free pamphlet "Dennis the Menace Takes a Poke at Poison," call the U.S. Food and Drug Administration at (301) 443-3170 or write to the FDA, Consumer Inquiry Staff, Room 1663, 5600 Fishers Lane, Rockville, MD 20857. Ask for their catalog of free publications for other parenting information, too.

☐ For a list of publications suggesting alternatives to toxic chemicals used in the home or garden, send a self-addressed, stamped envelope to Washington Toxics Coalition, 4516 University Way NE, Seattle, WA 98105.

☐ The following publications on poison prevention are available free from the U.S. Consumer Products Safety Commission: "First Aid Brochure," "Locked-up Poisons" (English and Spanish) and "Poison Lookout Checklist." Call (800) 638-CPSC or write: Office of Information and Public Affairs, U.S. Consumer Product Safety Commission, Washington, D.C. 20207.

☐ For information about how to recognize the symptoms of lead poisoning in your child and minimize risk of exposure, call the Alliance to End Childhood Lead Poisoning at (202) 543-1147 or send a self-addressed, stamped envelope to Alliance to End Childhood Lead Poisoning, 600 Pennsylvania Avenue SE, Suite 100, Washington, D.C. 20003, to receive brochures.

☐ The Maryland Department of the Environment will send you a packet of information on lead poisoning prevention and abatement. For the current cost and ordering information, call (410) 631-3859 or write to LPPD, 2500 Broening Highway, Baltimore, MD 21224.

☐ For the pamphlet "Reducing Exposure to Lead in Older Homes," send a self-addressed, stamped envelope to Washington Toxics Coalition, 4516 University Way NE, Seattle, WA 98105. You will receive their list of publications with prices and ordering information.

Other information about poisons is usually available free of charge from your local Poison Control Center. Look for the number of the center on the inside front cover of your phone book.

First-aid Supplies

☐ Check your supplies periodically and restock when necessary:

- antibiotic ointment to prevent infections in cuts
- antiseptic (ask your doctor for recommendation)
- assorted sizes of bandages:

  —butterfly bandages, which are excellent for closing small, clean cuts
  —1-inch and 2-inch rolls of sterile gauze bandages (for holding gauze dressings in place)
  —3-inch sterile gauze squares (for larger cuts and scrapes)
  —1-inch adhesive tape (for holding dressings or bandages in place)

- bicarbonate of soda (baking soda) to use for insect stings, heat rash, itching
- children's acetaminophen
- cotton balls (for applying ointments)
- ginger ale or cola drinks (some doctors recommend for upset stomachs)

- hot-water bottle (to relieve stomachache, earache, etc.)
- hydrocortisone cream (½%)—to relieve itching
- hydrogen peroxide (3% solution)—for cleaning wounds and soaking bandages off
- oral electrolyte maintenance solution (use as directed after vomiting)
- rectal and oral thermometers
- roll of sterile absorbent cotton
- scissors (for cutting bandages and dressings to size)
- syrup of ipecac (to induce vomiting in case of poisoning). *Use only as directed, after calling your physician or the Poison Control Center.*
- tweezers (for removing splinters)
- vaporizer or humidifier
- ice pack in the freezer for bumps and stings

Keep all supplies out of the reach of children!
For further information on first-aid procedures, see pages 219–230.

GENERAL OBSERVATIONS

☐ Occasionally include books about hospitals at story time. Your child will then at least be familiar with hospital procedure in case he ever needs to be taken to one in an emergency. Reading these books also might be helpful if anyone he knows is in a hospital.

☐ Do not give aspirin in any form to children because of its suspected link to Reye's syndrome, which can develop after a viral infection such as the flu or chicken pox.

☐ When giving tablets, grind the pills up and mix into peanut butter or applesauce. Make sure all the food is consumed. But check with your doctor first. Some pills *must* be swallowed whole.

☐ If your child is taking an antibiotic, give him as much yogurt as possible. It helps prevent diarrhea.

☐ An allergic reaction to medications or the dyes in them can cause rashes and/or extreme agitation.

☐ When your child is vomiting frequently, stay with her and catch the vomit in a clean diaper or bowl. It's much less frightening than constantly rushing her to the bathroom.

☐ Dried banana bits are good snacks if your child has mild diarrhea.

☐ If your child refuses to urinate in a cup for a urine sample, stretch plastic food wrap over the bowl of your toilet at home, making sure it forms a well.

☐ Hollow-handle medicine spoons and plastic syringes are great for giving liquid medications to your child—so much easier than spoons! They're available at any drugstore.

☐ If your child won't take medicine, pretend to take the first spoonful.

☐ Use a measuring teaspoon, not a regular one, to administer medicine for correct, consistent dosage.

☐ All parents should take a first-aid course and a cardiopulmonary resuscitation (CPR) course, especially if you have a swimming pool or other body of water nearby.

☐ Splinters can be removed painlessly if you've numbed the spot with an ice cube.

☐ Occasionally take out an "invisible" splinter, so your child will be used to tweezers.

☐ Some children scream even louder when you try to put ice on a bump or wash out a cut, so use any opportunity to administer ice—even for the gentlest of bumps. The same goes for washing a tiny scrape. Then, when you really need to use first aid, your child won't be frightened by a treatment she's not used to.

☐ Ice pops can soothe mouth and tongue injuries.

☐ Large bags of frozen vegetables conform to the shape of a sprained limb or bumped head and can reduce the swelling.

☐ Relieve sore fingers by encouraging play in a sink filled with ice-cold water.

☐ For a very sore throat, serve "gelatin tea." Follow the directions for making gelatin, but use warm water and serve it as a drink.

☐ Use a lollipop as a tongue depresser when you want to look at a child's throat.

☐ If you stick a bit of one end of a plastic bandage to itself, you can pull it off easily later.

☐ With a waterproof marker, draw a kiss (star, etc.) on the bandage for extra comfort.

☐ Placing calamine or any lotion on a wiggly toddler is a challenge. Instead of using your hand, try a paintbrush and paint it on. It tickles and kids love it!

☐ Fill in the Medical Emergency Consent Form (see page 153) and make *plenty* of copies for sitters. Don't forget grandparents.

FOR MORE INFORMATION

☐ Contact your local American Red Cross chapter about child care courses near you. These courses might cover such topics as preventing childhood injuries, first aid, caring for ill children, or learning about child development. Check with them to see what's available locally that interests you.

☐ To learn how to perform CPR on children and prevent accidents, contact your local American Heart Association for information on their 6 to 8 hour course called "Pediatric Basic Life Support Course." They also have brochures on various health-related topics; ask for them.

☐ For a free pamphlet on Lyme Disease, write: Lyme Disease, Will Rogers Institute, 785 Mamaroneck Avenue, White Plains, NY 10605, or call (914) 761-5550.

☐ Call (914) 593-LYME for recorded information on Lyme Disease prepared by the Lyme Disease Support Group for Children.

☐ Vision problems can lead to school difficulties and sometimes loss of sight. For eye health and safety information, and a free home eye test for preschoolers, call the National Society to Prevent Blindness at (800) 331-2020.

☐ For a free booklet on amblyopia, send a business size, self-addressed, stamped envelope to American Academy of Ophthalmology, P.O. Box 7424, San Francisco, CA 94120-7424. Call them at (415) 561-8500 to find out if

they have a free brochure on an eye-related topic of
particular concern to you.

The Pediatrician

Many toddlers are afraid of going to the doctor. These tips
may help:

☐ *"We role-play doctor and patient at home with a toy stetho-
scope right before a visit to the doctor. This rehearsal is
preparation enough to prevent tears."*

☐ Let the child bring *his* doctor's kit to the doctor's office
to examine the doctor.

☐ Take your child when you go to your doctor, so she will
see it's something we all do.

☐ Plan a favorite activity for after the visit.

☐ Be as honest as you possibly can. Don't say something
won't hurt when you know it will.

☐ Let your child sit on your lap as much as possible.

☐ Ask the doctor or nurse to take measurements and do
weighing at the end of the examination if this part of the
exam is upsetting your child.

☐ Take crayons for the paper on the examining table.

☐ If your child doesn't take to the doctor by the age of
three, switch doctors. Some doctors are much better than
others when handling the fearful child.

☐ Before leaving the office, ask the doctor to phone in any
prescription for you so you won't have to wait at the
drugstore with a sick child.

The Dentist and Tooth Care

Because dental visits for a toddler usually involve no more than tooth counting, brushing and a free toothbrush, they are usually most pleasant for everyone involved. Dentists like to talk to parents in the child's first year to discuss dental hygiene and proper fluoride protection. Regular visits usually start in the child's third year.

☐ Call your dentist to see what the first visit will be like so you and your child will know what to expect.

☐ Schedule appointments in the morning when your child is rested, fed and happy.

☐ Have the child sit in your lap during the first examination.

☐ Your own good attitude toward the dentist and tooth care will influence your child's attitude—for life.

☐ Never allow your child to fall asleep sucking on a bottle containing milk, formula, fruit juice or sweetened liquids. Put only water in your child's naptime or bedtime bottle.

☐ If a baby tooth is knocked out, save the tooth for the dentist to check and make sure that a piece of root does not remain in the gum.

☐ See pages 119–120 for toothbrushing tips.

☐ For more information about your children's dental health, ask your dentist for the latest information from the American Dental Association, the American Academy of Pediatric Dentistry and the American Society of Dentistry for Children.

Illness at Home

STAYING IN BED

☐ Give the child some kind of noisemaker (a birthday horn, bell, whistle) so he can call you if he really needs you.

☐ Don't leave medication where the child can reach it, but make sure all necessary supplies (tissues, wastebasket, bowl if child is vomiting) are within easy reach.

☐ Drawing, coloring and eating in bed will be easier to do on a breakfast tray. If you don't have one, support a piece of wood with large cans, bricks or boxes on either side. Or cut a cardboard box to fit. Or try your ironing board next to the bed.

☐ Firm chair or sofa cushions give a child more support for sitting than soft pillows.

☐ When food is served, a plastic tablecloth under the tray will catch spills.

☐ Bendable straws make drinking in bed much easier.

☐ Move the TV to the child or the child to the TV.

☐ When you must leave your child to make dinner or attend to other chores, set a timer so she'll know when you're coming back.

☐ Most children of this age will not stay in bed unless they're very ill. Check with your doctor; you will usually be advised to keep the child quiet but not necessarily in bed.

STAYING HAPPY

☐ Fill shoeboxes with different arts and crafts materials. One could contain macaroni to string and color; another, stickers and blank paper, another, sparkles and glue. Switch them frequently so the child doesn't tire of any one activity.

☐ Children love special toy treats, but they don't have to be new. You've probably got some baby toys stashed away that you can take out.

☐ Keep the child company and accomplish something at the same time: Give her room a thorough cleaning.

☐ Changing locations during the day is a great morale booster. Ask your doctor if you can take the child outside if the weather is mild.

☐ Surprises at mealtime make it more enjoyable. Consider hiding a piece of gum on the tray for the child to find or including a vase of flowers. Or have pudding for breakfast, eggs for dinner.

☐ If he dictates letters to grandparents and friends, he'll probably receive prompt responses by mail.

☐ You and your child can keep busy making seasonal decorations for the sickroom.

☐ Promise to read a story every hour.

☐ Music boxes with moving figures and wind-up musical crib toys are good for quiet amusement.

Hospital Emergency Rooms

☐ Do you know where your child's medical records are in case of an emergency? Fill out the charts on pages 233–234 and keep them near the phone (or in the car) so you can grab them quickly to take to the hospital.

☐ Call your local hospital to see if they give a tour of the hospital for preschoolers. If your child is familiar with the hospital, it will greatly reduce trauma in case of an emergency. Suggest this as a field trip for any preschool group your child may belong to. And children will love it; they are fascinated by hospitals.

☐ If your child has had a serious injury, don't try to drive her to the hospital yourself. She might vomit, faint or go into shock, and you couldn't handle that if you're driving. Call the police or an ambulance instead.

☐ If you must take your child to the hospital in an emergency, call your pediatrician and see if he or she can meet you there. Not only will the pediatrician be able to supply medical information if necessary, but it will be comforting to your child to see two familiar faces.

☐ Most emergency rooms have board-certified plastic surgeons on call. Ask for one if your child needs stitches on the face. Be firm; it is your right to request and get a plastic surgeon, although the emergency-room staff rarely suggests it and may even try to talk you out of it. Although deep cuts look awful, they can usually wait around 10 hours to be stitched. It's much worse to undo suture scars than to wait and have the surgery done properly. A general surgeon can certainly handle cuts on the rest of the body, but if you are concerned about scars, a plastic surgeon will probably do the best job—and the most expensive one.

Hospitalization

☐ Before your child enters the hospital:

- Go on a hospital tour.
- Read books about hospitals and operations. (Ask your children's librarian for recommendations.)
- From a pediatric nurse: *"One of a child's biggest fears is that she won't wake up after the operation. Use a stuffed animal (I use a monkey like Curious George) to show her how she will relax and go into a special kind of sleep . . . then wake up! Talk to your doctor about the procedures that will be followed, and discuss them with your child (in a playful, positive way) for a few days before she enters the hospital."*
- Don't tell the child about the hospitalization *too* far in advance. Four days is plenty.

☐ When you arrive at the hospital, there is usually a long wait with many forms to fill out before you can take your child to his room. Be sure to bring something to amuse him with.

☐ Don't buy special night clothes. Your child will have to wear hospital gowns.

☐ Insist on staying night and day in the room with your child. Nothing will make her feel better or get well faster than that. You and your spouse can take turns spending the night.

☐ If you can't be there 24 hours a day, make a tape of family voices singing, telling stories and so on and ask the nurses to play it for the child.

☐ If you have to leave him, draw a clock on a paper plate with movable hands attached with a brass fastener. Set the hands to the time when you'll be back and have him compare them to a clock.

☐ Leave a list of the child's bedtime routines and words for "potty."

☐ Help out as much as possible with the child's care (baths, feeding, putting him to bed).

☐ Parents can't always go to the operating floor with their child. Check this out and prepare your child.

☐ A pillowcase from home will cheer your child, as will a few of her favorite toys and pictures of family members and pets.

☐ Do bring the play doctor's kit from home, so your child can give the doctors and nurses shots, too.

5

At Home

The Child's Bedroom

☐ Build a simple platform for the crib mattress when your child wants to leave the crib for a bed. Your child can use this platform bed for another year or two, and it leaves more room for play than a regular bed would.

☐ In a long, narrow room use the back of a dresser as a headboard for the bed. If you have room, put another dresser at the bottom of the bed.

☐ In a small room install a top bunk bed but use the space under it for a desk/play area. Be sure the bed has a side rail.

☐ Install a dimmer switch for the overhead light. It can then double as a night-light that will not cast scary shadows as some night-lights do. Also, you can adjust the lighting easily if you must give medicine at night or just want to check on your sleeping child.

☐ Hang wastebaskets and diaper pails on the walls. It keeps children from plundering the contents and saves back strain.

☐ Instead of a bed, use a futon (a mattress that rolls up). Store it during the day, and the bedroom turns into a playroom. This is a good idea for two children who share a bedroom and need the play space.

☐ Consider investing in a trundle bed for these reasons:

- The lower mattress can be left pulled out to cushion any falls.
- It gives the parent a place to sleep if the child is ill or frightened.
- It's a built-in guest bed.

☐ Store a twin-bed mattress under the bed. It serves the same purpose as a trundle; it's just not as easy to get in and out.

☐ Cover a new mattress with a waterproof mattress cover right away if you want to keep it clean and fresh.

☐ Decorate your child's room with delightful, modestly priced posters celebrating the joy of reading. To receive a newsletter listing available materials, send a self-addressed, stamped envelope to Newsletter, Children's Book Council, 568 Broadway, Suite 404, New York, NY 10012.

☐ Cover the walls with your child's artwork.

☐ Paint the bottom half of the door with blackboard paint for a convenient chalkboard.

☐ Put up a bulletin board and use it as a "clearing center" for single socks, stray toy parts, medication schedules, birthday cards, pictures of relatives who are far away and anything else you can think of.

Around the House

☐ Use the playpen for a toddler who wants to play with blocks undisturbed by an inquisitive younger sibling.

☐ A sheet on the floor works well as a portable play area for using play dough, having picnics or tea parties. When play time is over, just shake out the sheet.

☐ A child-size table and chairs in the kitchen are handy for painting, cooking activities, working with play dough and so on.

☐ Store messy stuff such as play dough and paint on top of the refrigerator. It's easy to take down for play in the kitchen but inaccessible to little ones.

☐ A toddler will appreciate a box of toys in each room, which stays there. It's a snap to toss them all back in when you want to have a tidy room, and they don't get dragged all over the house.

☐ If your tot is forever pulling the knobs off your TV, dishwasher, stereo and so on, attach something repellent to them to remind the child not to touch. One mother used rubber bugs.

☐ If you live in a bilevel home, keep a basket at the foot of the stairs and throw small items that belong upstairs into it. Take the basket upstairs once or twice a day.

☐ To avoid smashed fingers, hook your doors *open* with a simple hook-and-eye attachment.

Toy Storage

☐ Cleanup will be that much easier if you make it a rule that water-play toys stay in the bathroom, blocks stay in the playroom and construction toys stay outside.

☐ Have just a few toys out at a time and change them periodically. It's confusing if there are too many around. Children like to scatter them but will not really play with them.

☐ Store various toys in boxes and take them out on different days of the week. This keeps parts of toys together and makes old toys seem exciting again.

☐ Put all the odd bits and pieces of toys you find in one bottle or box. Then there's only one place to look for a missing part.

☐ To find something that is lost, suggest that the child relax and close his eyes for a few moments before he renews his search. This will often jog his subconscious memory.

☐ Empty baby-wipes boxes and coffee cans are great for storing puzzle pieces and small toy parts.

☐ Shelves for toy storage are almost essential. Have a designated place for each toy or toy group. Make sure the shelves are attached securely to the walls to prevent any climbing accidents.

☐ Use clear plastic boxes when storing toys on shelves so the child can easily see the toy she wants and take it down.

☐ Keep some toys in baskets or boxes. These can be dumped out and all put back at the end of the day. But keep expensive toys, puzzles and toys with many pieces on high shelves and take one down at a time.

☐ Television carts are great for large items such as a dollhouse or record player.

☐ Hang up mesh hammocks for big toys and stuffed animals.

☐ Sew mesh, organza or sheer curtains into drawstring bags to hold toys with small parts. These can be hung in a closet, and your child can see the contents without dumping them on the floor.

☐ Shoe bags made of transparent plastic are great for holding toys; everything is always visible.

☐ Stacking vegetable bins are excellent for organizing everything from toys to clothes. They come in bright colors, too, and you can get wheels for them.

☐ Empty milk crates or laundry baskets are useful for toy storage. Each should have a sign with words and pictures indicating what belongs in it. This way children can put their own toys away and learn to recognize words.

☐ Toy chests are dangerous. Lids can slam down on heads and fingers. Worse, a child can be very frightened if trapped inside with another child sitting on the lid.

☐ Consider using that empty space under your stairs as a toy closet.

Clothing Storage

☐ Paste pictures of animals on the drawers of your child's dresser. Then you can ask your child to bring you socks from the "cat" drawer. Your child will be proud to be so independent. As he gets older, add numbers to the drawers and he'll learn his numbers as he learns neatness. Or you could tape pictures of the clothes themselves onto the drawers.

☐ Shelves work better than dresser drawers. You can quickly see what you've got and what you need. (How many times have you discovered something never worn and now outgrown in the bottom of a deep drawer?)

☐ A tension rod between the dresser and wall makes a practical, space-saving open closet.

☐ Create a closet rod for a child by hanging a dowel with heavy cord or wire from the existing closet rod.

☐ Cut your closets in half vertically. In one half install five or more shelves for toys and clothes storage, and use two rods for hanging clothes in the other half. This will *double* your space.

☐ Install a special coat rack at child level right by the back door (or on it). Children can be trained at a very early age to hang up their own coat and hat. A shelf above it can store mittens.

☐ Keep an "outgrown clothing basket" and deposit appropriate articles into it. Launder and store these things separately.

Chores

Although you don't want to burden your little ones with too much responsibility, there are some chores that are easy and fun for toddlers. Many children enjoy the following:

- Puffing up the bed pillows. Threes can help make the bed.
- Tearing up lettuce for salads.
- Putting napkins and silverware on the table and clearing same.
- Drying silverware and nonbreakable dishes.
- Sorting laundry and matching socks.
- Wiping the bathtub clean after a bath.
- Making sure the pets have water.
- Picking up at least some toys.
- Hanging up clothing.

To encourage cooperation, try these suggestions:

☐ You are much more likely to have success with an activity such as cleaning up if you do it *with* the toddler rather than expecting her to do it alone.

☐ Tell your child she has to pick up five (or whatever) toys during cleanup time, and then help count to five as she does it. You do the rest, but increase the number each day as cooperation increases.

☐ A little wagon will make it fun for your child to pick up the toys that are scattered around the house.

☐ Many children love vacuuming. Motivate them to clean their rooms by letting them vacuum after the toys are picked up. Sprinkle a bit of confetti on the floor so progress is visible.

☐ At cleanup time, put on marching music. It really seems to get things moving, especially if you challenge children to get the toys put away before the record is over.

☐ Treat chores as a game. Have a race to see who can get the blocks in the box faster.

☐ Making weekly chore lists with check-off boxes can help everyone in the family, but the little ones will be especially proud of their achievements. Stick-on stars are wonderful motivators when a job has been well done.

Television

Toddlers need to interact with their environment for optimum physical and psychological growth and development. Watching television takes them away from this essential activity. For your child's sake, limit access to the TV.

☐ If your child insists on watching TV four inches away from the screen (most children do), introduce a special TV seat—a minirocker, a booster seat, a piece of old carpeting, a pillow—anything to draw her farther back.

☐ Use TV as a jumping-off point for imaginative play. *"After watching an animal program where a cheetah chased an impala,"* one father reports, *"my son and I played 'cheetah and impala' for weeks. Guess who I got to be?"*

☐ As much as possible, watch television with your child. Explain and comment on what you see, especially the commercials. Children can learn at a very early age to be critical of what they see and hear on TV; otherwise they passively accept everything on TV as the truth.

☐ Be aware that many so-called children's shows are simply too scary for little ones (and some big ones). Always watch programs with your child and don't hesitate to turn the TV off if your child seems upset or if *you* are. You may hear howls of protest, but you may save your child many nightmares.

☐ If your child is watching too much TV, set a time limit per day and let the child have a voice in choosing the shows he wants to watch.

☐ Some TV sets come equipped with devices that can block out channels. You might want to consider this option if you're buying a new one.

☐ Try watching TV together without the sound on and talk about everything you see. Guess what will happen next.

☐ Have trouble turning the TV off without temper tantrums? Try turning the sound off first. Children quickly lose interest.

Environmental Activities

Encouraging a toddler to respect his environment is easy with a little forethought.

☐ Have your toddler sort recyclable items—paper, plastic and cans—into proper containers.

☐ Tell your child every time you reuse something for a craft project that you are doing something good for the environment.

☐ Make a terrarium out of a two-liter soda bottle. Collect moss, ferns and other plants in the woods.

☐ Your toddler can learn about family responsibility and recycling if he is responsible for dumping vegetable scraps in the outdoor compost pail.

☐ Show your child that water can be used more than once by watering plants with clean-rinse dishwater.

☐ Make a bird feeder or buy a windowsill feeder that your child can fill with food.

☐ Let your child explore the world outdoors with a magnifying glass.

☐ Teach shapes by cutting meat trays into circles, squares, triangles and so on. Or, cut meat trays into boat, fish or other aquatic shapes for bath or pool toys.

☐ Visit or join your local Nature Conservancy or Wildlife Preserve. Many have special programs for preschool children.

☐ Plant a garden inside or out. Marigolds are particularly resilient to small hands; patio tomatoes, sweet cherry tomatoes, beets, pumpkins, zucchini squash, peas, beans and herbs are easy to grow and are very satisfying for toddlers.

   Grow tomatoes and marigolds together in tubs or pots if garden space is limited. Marigolds are natural insect repellents for tomatoes.

☐ Give your child one of the special nature gifts listed on page 206.

FOR MORE INFORMATION

☐ For a free reprint of "Backyard Habitat" published by the National Wildlife Federation, call (800) 432-6564. They can also give you information on "My Big Backyard," a nature magazine for three- to five-year-olds.

Clothing and Laundry

Underwear

- [ ] Underwear always seems to shrink. Buy it two sizes too large.

- [ ] Little girls who insist on nightgowns in the winter will be warmer if they're also wearing long underwear.

- [ ] Summer tops can be winter undershirts; put them to use before they're outgrown.

Shirts, Sweaters, Tops

- [ ] Avoid white collars and stripes on colorful children's shirts. The white will get spotted and you'll have a hard time bleaching it.

- [ ] Remove fuzz from sweaters by shaving the surface lightly with a razor.

- [ ] Don't buy shirts that have to be tucked into pants. They never are. Those shirts that come as part of a pants/vest outfit will always end up hanging out below the vest.

Pants, Overalls, Dresses

☐ Pants with elastic waists droop with diapers, get soaked easily (they act like a wick), hang down below fat tummies and generally look sloppy. Buy them for toilet training and/or toilet-trained children. Overalls look best on diapered toddlers.

☐ Prevent holes at the knees by ironing on patches inside the pants when they're new.

☐ Corduroy is a nice fabric, but it wears quickly at the knees if you have a child who is hard on pants. Then it looks terrible, and there's nothing you can do about it.

☐ Don't bother to hem pants that are too long; rolled-up cuffs are in style.

☐ Use suspenders or elasticized belts if pants are too big around the waist.

☐ Sew rickrack or other fancy trim over hemline lines that show after you've lengthened pants or dresses. Or disguise them by tracing over the hemline with a felt marker that matches the color of the garment.

☐ Lengthen pants by sewing a fancy trimming or preshrunk grosgrain ribbon to the cuffs.

☐ You'll get much more use out of overalls if you buy those brands that have extralong straps with buttons that can be moved as your child grows.

☐ Add a bit of elastic to each overall strap. There will be more room for growth, and the straps won't slide off.

☐ Cut off the legs of overalls or pants to make them into shorts for summer.

Sleepwear

☐ When pajama sleepers become too short, cut off the feet and sew on knitted slippers or socks. Put iron-on patches on the bottom of socks for longer wear and better traction.

☐ Buy multiple pairs of the same pajamas. Then there will be no arguments about which ones to wear, and if the bottoms get wet and have to be washed, you'll always have another that matches.

☐ Two-piece pajamas are most practical for the child who is learning to sleep through the night without diapers. If he has to urinate, they're easy to pull down, and if they get wet, only the bottom has to be removed.

☐ *"I find pajamas too skimpy and expensive. Use T-shirts and old sweatpants or T-shirts and underpants in warm weather."*

Winter Wear

☐ One-piece snowsuits are much easier to put on than suits with pants and a jacket. One big zip and it's done. On the other hand, you'll have to buy an extra jacket for warmer days.

☐ You'll get an extra year's wear out of a jacket or snowsuit by sewing knitted cuffs (you can get these in dime stores or at a notions counter, or cut the cuffs off discarded sweaters) to the sleeves when they get too short.

☐ If your child has outgrown the sleeves on his winter jacket, cut them off and turn the jacket into a warm vest.

☐ Buy mitten/glove clips (available in children's clothing stores) to keep mittens permanently attached to jackets.

☐ Avoid losing mittens by sewing a piece of yarn to each mitten and threading them through the sleeves. (Note: When your child is old enough to put on his own coat, the clip method works better than this, as the child can get tangled in the yarn.)

☐ Knot the ends of the drawstring in hoods so they won't get pulled out. Or sew the drawstring to the middle of the hood. If the string does come out, attach a safety pin to one end and work it back through.

Shoes and Boots

☐ Sandpaper the soles to keep them from slipping. Or tape on some adhesive tape in a T shape (with the cross of the T near the toe).

☐ Crayons and felt markers can quickly touch up scuff marks.

☐ Cleaning fluid will remove many stains from children's shoes.

☐ When the ends come off shoelaces, apply clear nail polish or short pieces of tape.

☐ Everybody in the world has red boots. Make your child's boots distinctive with colored tape designs, stick-on dots or decals.

☐ Boots slip on easily if you put a plastic bag over your child's shoe. Use the plastic bags you put fruit into at the supermarket, or plastic newspaper bags.

Buttons and Zippers

☐ Use heavy-duty waxed thread or waxed dental floss to sew on buttons that will stay on.

☐ Use elastic thread so your child can button easier.

☐ Avoid reversible garments. The zippers are a pain for you and your child.

☐ The larger the zipper pull, the easier it will be for your child to zip himself.

Reluctant Dressers

☐ A wiggly child will quiet down and let you dress him if you tell him a story with lots of suspense that lasts until you've tied the final shoelace.

☐ Kiss and wave good-bye to hands and feet as they disappear in sleeves, socks and shoes. Say hello when they reappear.

☐ Put on shoes and socks while the child is in the high chair, or set him on the kitchen counter. He can't run away from you.

☐ Sit on your child (gently) and dress him. *"I did this once out of desperation, and he hated it so that the mere threat of it brought cooperation."*

☐ Playact with a favorite doll or stuffed animal. When dressing time arrives, say "Teddy bear wants to see you take off your shirt." Be sure Teddy claps when the child performs!

☐ Give your child a flashlight instead of a toy to distract him. He can do so many different things with the light that it's a distraction that will work for years.

☐ Listen to a favorite record while dressing, but explain that it will be turned off if cooperation ceases.

☐ Ask the child the name or color of each garment that you put on or take off.

☐ Dress the child in front of a mirror.

☐ Cover your face with the top of the turtleneck, give the child the large open bottom and say "Where's Mommy?" To see you she has to put her head into the opening and pull it on.

☐ Let the child choose between two outfits.

☐ Refer to clothes in a special way, such as "Let's wear Grandma's shirt today."

☐ Tell your child how good he will look once he's ready. Then take him to a mirror and show him.

☐ A child who refuses to wear mittens will often be happy to wear warm, fuzzy puppets on her hands.

☐ Knit booties (the kind that don't kick off) make good emergency mittens.

☐ Take a calendar to the refrigerator and let your child stick or draw a star on each day that she dresses without a fuss.

☐ Have the child race with his brother, sister, a song, a record or a timer.

Teaching Children to Dress Themselves

☐ Point out labels, zippers and the like as clues to determine the front and back of a garment. If there is none, make some with a laundry marker.

☐ Use costumes and dress-up clothes to teach a child how to dress. *"My son learned how to put on his Superman outfit in no time flat."*

☐ A child needs *plenty* of time to dress when she's doing it herself. Remember that to a three-year-old, this is a tremendous task; buttons, for instance, can take three to four minutes each.

☐ Teach your child to button herself from the bottom up, so the buttons will match the right buttonhole.

☐ Mark either the right or left shoe in a special, consistent way.

☐ Have your child watch as you put his shoes together and mark on the inside edge of both. Then tell him that when the marks are next to each other, the shoes will be on the correct feet.

☐ How can a child tell his left hand from the right? When he puts his hands palms down on a table, the outspread thumb makes an *L*.

☐ Buy only tube socks (without heels) to make putting on socks easy.

☐ Make sure all neck holes are loose-fitting and go over your child's head easily before you buy. *Nothing* is more frustrating to a beginner than getting her head stuck.

☐ To enlarge the neck hole, slit the shoulder seam, cover the raw edges with bias tape and sew on a snap.

☐ Buy only solid-color pants with shirts that match so children can pick their own shirt and pants and always look good.

☐ Teach your child the nursery-school method of putting coats on: Lay the coat on the floor on its back, with the arms and back at the child's feet. The child sticks both arms in the sleeves and flips it over his head. Once it is mastered, this method makes the child feel super-independent. (See illustration.)

☐ Tots can zip much more easily if there is a big paper clip attached to the end of the zipper.

☐ Use Velcro strips to replace fasteners on overalls or anything else your child is having difficulty fastening.

☐ *"I bought a small doll that had a zipper, buttons, shoelaces and snaps for my daughter to play with. As she mastered each task, she was given a fancy certificate to display on the refrigerator."*

Keeping Clothes Clean

☐ Spray white collars and light-color shirts with fabric protector so that spills will bead instead of becoming absorbed.

☐ Soak garments in cold water with a bit of white vinegar added to prevent colored fabrics from running.

☐ Use baking soda with bleach to take away the odor of the bleach.

☐ You can throw cloth sneakers into the washing machine along with the rest of the laundry (but only with similar colors). Allow laces to dangle from one hole only. Air-dry to avoid shrinkage.

☐ For a homemade spot cleaner, mix equal amounts of dishwashing liquid and ammonia. Store this mixture in an empty squeeze bottle (label it) and apply to spots before clothes go into the washing machine. (Do not wash with chlorine bleach when you do this.)

☐ An ice cube will freeze gum on clothes, hair and elsewhere so you can peel it off. Or stick the gummy clothing in the freezer for a while.

☐ Peanut butter removes gum from hair. Rub it in to loosen the gum and slide it off.

☐ Line-dry T-shirts with iron-on decals; the decals shrink and tear in the dryer.

☐ Dust baby powder on spots on white clothes. It won't get rid of the stain, but they will look better.

Stain Removal

☐ The proper time to deal with a stain is *immediately*! The longer you wait, the more difficult it will be to remove it. Remember, once the stain is set, it can be difficult to remove completely.

☐ Before applying any stain remover directly on the affected spot, experiment with it on some portion of the garment that is not visible just to make certain that the remover is safe for the fabric.

☐ If you are unable to treat a stain immediately, soak the stain in water, put soap on it, place the garment in a plastic bag and freeze it until you have some free time.

☐ Keep a solid stain treatment stick by the hamper and treat stains before you put the clothes in the hamper.

☐ Put the laundry in the machine to soak overnight with detergent or a commercial presoak. Wash it in the morning. This method will take care of most stains.

☐ Make sure stains are out before putting clothes in the dryer. Dryer heat sets stains in.

☐ The most popular method of removing really tough stains is to mix a soaking solution of automatic dishwasher detergent, bleach and water. There doesn't seem to be agreement as to the proportions of bleach to water to detergent. Try this recipe first, and if it doesn't do the trick, increase the bleach or detergent or soaking time.
    ½ cup bleach
    ½ cup automatic dishwasher detergent
    1 gallon hot water

Soak overnight, then wash as usual. Remember, this is a last resort. If you are concerned about fading, test the garment first. Also, the dishwasher detergent will actually break down fibers, and the treated garment will not last as long as it would have.

☐ Use the following guide for removing common (to some of us, anyway!) stains.

BLOOD

- Blood and protein stains need to be treated as quickly as possible. Scrape off excess substance, then soak the fabric in *cold* water with enzyme presoak for at least 30 minutes. Wash, then dab with bleach or diluted hydrogen peroxide. (Test for color fastness first.) Treat any remaining spots by rubbing with a paste made from detergent and water. Wash again.
- For a small spot, rub immediately with saliva. This is an old quilter's trick that helps when you prick your finger with a needle.

CRAYON

- Melt crayon marks out of clothes by covering the stain on both sides with paper towels and ironing. The heat will melt the wax into the toweling.

FRUIT AND VEGETABLE JUICE

- Stretch fabric over a bowl and pour boiling water through the stain from a height of about two feet.
- Or soak immediately in cold water. Wash with detergent, *not* soap. If the stain remains, rub it with liq-

uid nonchlorine bleach or a paste made from powdered oxygen bleach. Wait for 15 to 30 minutes and wash again.

GRASS

- Sponge with white vinegar or denatured alcohol. Rinse thoroughly.

PAINT

- Poster paints: Allow to dry and brush off. Rub liquid detergent directly on the stain before washing. (At home, mix your child's paints with soap flakes, then any mistakes will come right out in the wash.)
- Oil paint: Use paint remover.

URINE

- Soak in cold water, wash with detergent and then, if the stain has not been removed, sponge with mild ammonia solution (1 tbsp. ammonia, ½ tsp. liquid detergent, 1 qt. warm water). Rinse.

GREASE

- Immediately apply a prewash stain remover, following label directions carefully. Wash in the hottest water safe for the garment. Repeat the procedure if necessary.
- For black grease, rub solid shortening or vegetable oil on the stain, then scrape the fabric with your fingernail. The grease comes right off. Launder the garment in hot water to get the oil out.

General Observations

☐ Buy the best clothes you can if you're planning to pass them along.

☐ Choose a color theme (earth tones, pastels) for each season, and your child's clothes will always mix well.

☐ Choose a certain drawer (or box) for all the clothes you're given that are too large. Then each season go through it to see what will fit. Nothing's worse than suddenly finding a gorgeous sweater you put away and forgot about until it was too late.

☐ To make hand-me-downs seem special, always call them by names such as "nursery-school pants" or "a four-year-old's dress" (to a three).

☐ If you want to make clothes larger to use for one more season, soak them overnight in a gallon of hot water mixed with 1 cup of automatic dishwasher detergent. (Note: This will actually break down the fibers of the clothes, which makes them bigger, but the garments won't last as long.)

☐ When you have a day of winter sports ahead of you, keep snow out of children's mittens by tucking them inside the sleeves of the snowsuit and wrapping the wrists snugly with masking tape. This works for boots, too.

☐ When you undress your child, put socks (or anything very small) in a nylon net. Put the tied-up net in the washer with the rest of the laundry. This way the small things don't get jumbled up with the other clothes and are easy to find and sort. (Use the same method for keeping outgrown clothing that you want to wash once more and then store separately from the rest of the wash.)

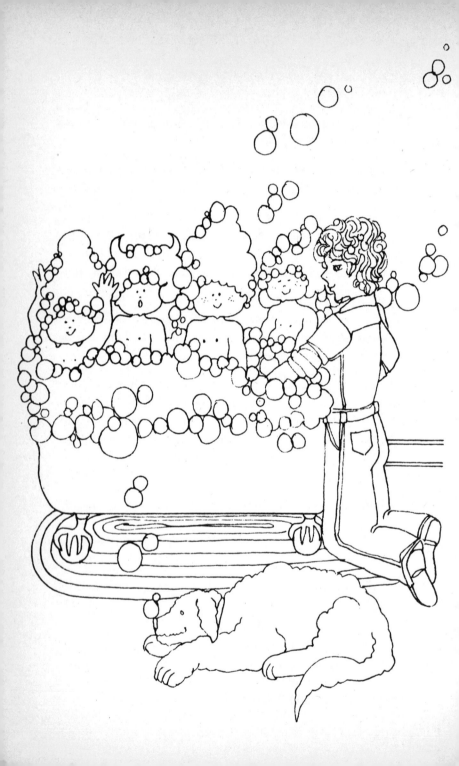

7

Keeping Clean and General Hygiene

Bath-time Fun

☐ Give your child a paintbrush to play with in the tub. A 2-inch trim brush is a good size.

☐ Aerosol foam soap is fun for children and gets them clean, too.

☐ Sponges cut into interesting shapes (animals, people, houses, etc.) make great bath toys.

☐ Save those old squirt or spray bottles for bathtub and sink play. (Be sure to clean them *thoroughly* first.)

☐ Occasionally let your toddler play with something from your kitchen, such as your big spaghetti pot, wire whisk or cupcake tin.

☐ If you have a bad back or just a temporary back problem, use your laundry tub for baths.

☐ Children will let you wash them if you make or buy puppet washcloths and say such things as "Grover wants to kiss you under the chin (ears, toes, etc.)." Most children like to have their own puppets for cleaning their favorite toy.

☐ If children resist ear washing, shampooing and the like, simply start to take them out of the tub. They usually love their bath so much that they will relent.

☐ Let your toddler take a shower sometimes. Babies are often fearful of showers, but after a summer or two of sprinkler play, a shower is often a welcome treat for a toddler.

☐ If your child is afraid of the tub, get in with him until he loses his fear.

☐ Many twos will suddenly become afraid of disappearing down the drain, so pull the plug after the child is out of the tub.

☐ Toddlers get rambunctious in the tub, so use a *large* rubber mat in the bottom of the tub (or glue-on stickers) to prevent falls.

☐ Be wary of bubble bath. Certain brands can sting the genital area badly.

☐ Use plastic onion bags to hang tub toys to drain after use.

Shampoo Resistance

The hand-held shower attachment is the most popular solution to shampooing problems. It is really worth installing if you are encountering consistent resistance. Not only does it make wetting and rinsing much faster and easier, but best of all, your child will love to play with it. *"Shampooing is no longer a problem because my son is allowed to play with the sprayer attachment only* after *he's been shampooed. You can bet that the shampoo gets finished in record time."* Be sure to close the shower curtain *tight* before you let your child loose with the sprayer.

- ☐ Dilute the baby shampoo. It makes rinsing faster and easier.

- ☐ Do the shampooing first and get it over with so she has the tub toys to look forward to. Don't save it till last and end on an unhappy note.

- ☐ Find another child (preferably older) who likes shampoos, and bathe them together a few times. Don't put pressure on your child to be like another, but the other child's delight in washing hair might just transfer.

- ☐ Use a squirt bottle for dispensing shampoo. It's easier to control the amount of shampoo used.

- ☐ Use a plant mister to wet hair without too much trauma. *After* hair is wet, the child can play with the mister.

- ☐ Give your child a mirror so he can watch you shape his soapy hair into animal ears or Batman horns.

- ☐ Get your child blowing bubbles. It will keep her busy while you wash her hair.

- ☐ Put a stripe of petroleum jelly across the toddler's forehead to deflect drips of water.

☐ Buy a doll with hair your child can shampoo. This can really work wonders to relieve anxiety.

☐ Give your toddler a washcloth to hold during the shampoo. He'll feel so much better if he can wipe his own eyes.

☐ If your child knows a poem or song, have her recite or sing while you wash her hair. It will hold her attention and keep her chin up.

☐ If your child really hates it when *you* shampoo his hair, ask someone else to do it for a while. *"My son got so he cried only when I washed his hair,"* said one mother.

☐ When shampooing, lean the child back, support his head with your arm and hold his shoulder. This keeps water out of his face and he feels very secure. Tell the child that you remember this was the way he *loved* to have his hair washed when he was a baby. Stress this point.

☐ Try swimming goggles or face mask on the child who fears shampoo or water in her eyes. This will leave a bit of the hair unshampooed (under the strap), but better some than none. If it works, you might convince her to hold the goggles on next time so she won't have to use the strap. Make sure that during the summer you point out all the "big kids" who wear goggles; that will make them seem extra desirable. Get your child to use them in the pool, and you'll have no problems at home.

☐ Shampoo at the kitchen sink with the spray attachment. The child lies faceup on the counter while you wash and rinse.

☐ Rinse hair with a watering can.

☐ If your child is bothered by water in the ear, try ear plugs. Or buy the plastic ear caps used by hairdressers to protect ears under the dryer.

☐ When rinsing hair, fold the top of the child's ear forward and water won't run in.

☐ Take your toddler along when you go to the beauty parlor. Show her how the women get their hair washed and emphasize what fun it all is. Then play Beauty Parlor next time you want to shampoo.

☐ Some children feel more secure during the rinsing stage if they put their elbows on the edge of the tub and hold a cloth over their eyes as they tilt their head back.

☐ Have the child look up at the shower. Then gently cover his eyes with a washcloth. Pour water over his head with a cup, and soapy water will go down his back.

☐ *"The imaginary 'bathroom bug' lives on the ceiling above our tub. As we begin the shampoo, I ask my son what our bug looks like today, the color of his spots, what he's doing, and so on and as I wash and rinse, he continues to look straight up at the ceiling to report on the bug's doings."*

☐ To get your child to put his head back during the rinse, put a large decal (available at many baby stores) on the ceiling above the tub and talk about it.

☐ Use the shower to rinse her hair.

☐ Tell him you need 10 cupfuls for a rinse, and then count as you rinse. Knowing when the rinsing will be over makes it bearable.

☐ Some children are much happier if they pour the water over their own heads to rinse the shampoo.

☐ *"Our son firmly resisted hair washing until he discovered that he could rinse his own hair by lying back in the bath and (with help) lowering his head into the water."*

☐ Children are often intrigued by the sounds they hear when their ears are underwater, so if you can get them to float on their backs and listen, you can also rinse without much problem.

☐ An older child can help you out. *"My older son invented the story of the 'dirty yuckies' that lived in my younger son's hair, but shampoo and water took care of them. Now my youngest had a reason for washing his hair and was much more cooperative."*

☐ Use a baby hair conditioner after shampooing your toddler's hair to avoid all those tears during combing. Be sure to comb while the hair is still wet.

☐ Some children will happily get a shampoo at the hairdresser's and nowhere else.

Hair Care

☐ Comb or brush hair while the child is in the high chair.

☐ Separate long, tangly hair with your fingers before you comb or brush.

☐ Let your toddler comb your hair before you comb his.

☐ Comb or brush tangled hair from the bottom up, a little bit at a time. Brushing from the top down just mushes the tangles together and makes them worse.

☐ Count strokes as you brush. When children join in the counting, they forget the brushing, and it teaches them numbers.

☐ A collection of colorful barrettes can be an incentive for a little girl who resists a hairbrush. Let her choose which clips she wants to put on after her hair has been brushed.

CUTTING HAIR AT HOME

☐ Play Barber. Put a chair in front of a mirror and pin a towel around the child's neck. A boy might like a pretend shave after he gets his hair cut.

☐ Tape bangs down with special hair tape (it doesn't pull the hair) and cut above or below for a very neat line. (The tape can be bought at any drugstore.)

☐ Invest in a pair of haircutting scissors. They're very sharp and will result in a good, quick cut.

☐ Cut your toddler's bangs and hair around the ears first while he's relatively still. Use rounded-tip baby scissors for safety.

☐ Watch carefully when your child gets a professional hair cut. You'll learn some good techniques.

☐ Sprinkle powder on the child's neck after the cut, and all that itchy hair can be brushed away easily.

Hand Washing

☐ Animal-shape soap makes hand washing more enjoyable.

☐ A soap pump is easier and more fun to use than a bar of soap.

☐ Toddlers clean their hands willingly if it means playing in a sink full of bubbles created by a small squirt of dishwashing liquid, shampoo or bubble bath.

☐ If you encounter persistent resistance to washing hands before meals, let your child "wash the dishes" at the sink while you make lunch or dinner. Supply a stool, soapy water and plastic cups, and the hands will be clean in no time.

Toothbrushing

☐ To set a good example, always brush your teeth when you brush the child's teeth. You could even make a family game out of it and brush together around the sink.

☐ Brushes can sometimes hurt toddler gums. Use a moistened gauze pad instead to wipe the teeth clean.

☐ Toothbrushing a problem? Buy a bunch of brushes and let your child choose the toothbrush he wants to use that night. A little bit of control goes a long way.

☐ Buy a small (travel-size) tube of toothpaste for your child and he'll know it's his very own. *"This made a big difference to my child,"* reported one mom. Buy three in different colors and flavors and he may never come out of the bathroom.

☐ Let your child brush your teeth first.

☐ Place a mirror at the child's eye level so he can see himself brush.

☐ Count her teeth as you brush.

☐ To get your toddler to open his mouth *wide*, teach him Tarzan yells.

☐ Make it a rule that if your children want candy they must brush their teeth right after eating it.

☐ *"I solved the toothbrushing problem by drawing a furry bug and telling my children that this was a germ that lived on the food in their teeth. If they didn't brush, he would stay in their mouths. That did it."*

☐ Pretend your child's teeth are so shiny after brushing that they hurt your eyes. She'll love chasing you around the house trying to show you her shiny teeth.

☐ Give your child a toothbrush when you're reading a story or when she's watching TV. Just chewing on it helps clean teeth.

☐ Tablets are available at drugstores that, when chewed after brushing, temporarily stain all the parts the brush has missed. Not only will your child enjoy checking her own teeth, but she will also love pointing out the places *your* toothbrush missed.

8

Sleeping

Getting children to bed and keeping them there is no easy task, especially after the switch has been made from the crib to a regular bed. But it's important for parents to remember that almost all children from ages two to five have sleeping disturbances at one time or another. Some children strenuously resist going to bed; others have great difficulty falling asleep. Some wake up frequently from nightmares, while others insist on special nightly rituals. Here are suggestions from parents who have coped with it *all*.

Naps

☐ A nap routine is as important as a bedtime routine. Read a story, tuck a doll in bed or sing a special song, but be consistent. It will help your child relax and fall asleep.

☐ If your child really resists a nap, insist on a quiet time in his room anyway. (After all, it's *you* who need the break.) A long-playing record is a good quiet-time activity.

☐ Set the timer so she'll know when the nap/quiet time is over if she can't sleep.

☐ If the after-lunch nap habit has been broken for some reason, try taking him out in the car after lunch to get him to fall asleep. Once he's back to sleeping at that hour, it will be easier to nap at home.

☐ A special toy, brought out only at nap time, will keep a child happy and in his room.

☐ A gate on the door will remind your child not to come out of the room until nap time is over.

☐ *"My child almost always goes to sleep if I do,"* reports one mother. *"It's the best way I know of to get an erratic napper to sleep when he really needs it. I tell him he must be very quiet and not disturb me until a certain time. I guess the lack of stimulation bores him to sleep."*

☐ Play Camp-Out at nap time. Give your child a blanket and pillow and tell her she may sleep anywhere for her nap.

☐ Don't wash the dishes or do other chores during the child's nap that you could do with the child. Use those precious minutes for yourself!

☐ Wake the child by making noises in her room. If you approach her directly, you may bear the brunt of her crankiness until she's fully awake.

The Transition Phase

If your child is beginning to stay up too late at night, her sleep needs are probably changing and her nap schedule should be altered in some way. Because most toddlers resist change of any kind, you will have to be extra patient during this period. These tips may help during the transition phase, when she goes from two naps a day to one or drops napping altogether.

☐ Change mealtimes to ease the transition. When two naps merge into one in the middle of the day, lunch might have to be put off till later in the afternoon until the adjustment is made to an after-lunch nap.

☐ Because late afternoon is a cranky time anyway, especially when there's been no nap, serve dinner early. Don't be surprised if the child is too tired and fussy to feed himself; this will change as he adjusts to his new schedule.

☐ Try not to take your child out in the car after 3 P.M. if you possibly can in order to avoid the dreaded late nap that throws everybody's schedule off.

☐ If a late nap is unavoidable, wake the child after a half hour so she won't stay up past her bedtime. If she's cranky, a bath will soothe her.

☐ Being read to, listening to records or watching TV are all things that will help your child rest and recharge without sleeping.

☐ If your child really wants her nap, she'll fall asleep no matter what you do. Remember that you are just helping and trying to make it easier; it's up to her to make the change.

Bedtime Routines

☐ Start your routine at least a half hour before bedtime. Active and excitable twos and threes need time to calm down.

☐ If your child won't stay in her bedroom and go to sleep but keeps coming out to bother you, tell her you are going to go to bed, but she can stay up. Chances are she'll go right to bed once the game has ended.

☐ *"We set the timer for 10 minutes before our daughter's bedtime. She then has our undivided attention, but when the timer dings, it's time for bed."*

☐ Denying a bedtime story for really obnoxious behavior may cause an hour's worth of crying, but bedtime behavior after that will improve greatly.

☐ Let the child read in bed or play quietly with toys and calm *himself* down after the final good night.

☐ Cut out all cola drinks near bedtime. (Many contain caffeine.)

☐ Avoid looking at pictures of animals such as gorillas in magazines or anything else that might possibly be scary or lead to nightmares. Photographs of wild animals, which can be enjoyed during the day, are often upsetting at night.

☐ A gate on the door reminds a child that she must stay in her room after bedtime.

☐ To keep a child *in* bed once you've put him to bed, try lying down with him for a few minutes after you turn out the light. This relaxes some children enough to let them drift off to sleep.

☐ Favorite bedtime stories are often those you make up with your child as the main character. It's a good way to review the day, reinforce any lessons learned and emphasize all the good, positive feelings you have toward each other.

☐ Block out outside noises for light sleepers by recording a humming sound (hair dryer, fan, vacuum cleaner) on a cassette and playing it on a tape recorder in your child's room while she goes to sleep.

☐ Try this relaxation technique with a very keyed-up child: Have him lie in bed on his back, eyes closed. Touch his feet and tell them to go to sleep in a quiet, soothing voice. Repeat that for his knees, legs, and move up his whole body.

☐ Listening to a story cassette in bed relaxes some children after you leave them in their rooms. If the cassette is double-sided, dub it onto a longer-playing cassette so there is no need to flip the tape in the middle of the story.

☐ Prevent endless requests for water by leaving a small Thermos or camping canteen filled with water in the child's room.

☐ *"Our two-year-old developed the exhausting habit of rising at 5:30 A.M. We bought him a small alarm clock and told him he couldn't get up till the alarm rings. By moving the alarm back by ten minutes every day, we are all in bed until 6:45 A.M. and much more rested."*

The Transition from Crib to Bed

Most children make this transition easily if they're prepared for it. Unless there's a baby on the way who needs the crib, most parents advise not rushing this major step. The older the child, the more quickly and happily she will adapt. Waiting until the child is three is often recommended.

☐ If you need the crib for a new baby, start the transition early in your pregnancy, so your toddler will be happy in his bed when the baby comes and there will be no feeling on his part that the baby has usurped his rightful place.

☐ Begin leaving the crib side down so the child can get in and out by himself. (He'll probably need a chair next to the crib to climb on.) Or just remove one side; the mattress frame on most cribs will secure the other three sides.

☐ Set up the new bed long before you intend to have your child use it. Many children will start napping in the bed by their own choice if it is there. Getting used to the bed this way makes the transition easy.

☐ Take your child with you to choose his new bed, and take his feelings about it into consideration. This will make him feel much more positive about the transition.

☐ New bedding (sheets with favorite cartoon characters, for example) is a good incentive for the move.

☐ Leave the crib set up after you bring in the bed and let the child choose between them. Don't dismantle the crib until the child is comfortable in his bed.

☐ *"We left the crib and the bed in the room for several weeks, and our son chose the bed for naps, the crib for nighttime. One day, when he was at school, I removed the crib and stored it away. I told him about it on the way home from school, showed him where it was stored and that was that."*

☐ Keep the crib set up in case you have problems. *"My daughter began to get out of the bed all the time, but she wouldn't climb out of the crib. We told her if she continued to get out of her bed at night, she would be put in the crib to sleep. She really wanted to be a big girl, and this warning settled her down."*

☐ Let the child help you dismantle the crib and put it away. If she resists this activity, you'll know she's not ready for sleeping in a bed.

Please note: If your toddler isn't ready for the transition but there's a baby due soon, you'll either have to put the baby temporarily in a portacrib or get another crib. Look at it as an investment in your children's future relationship. Save money and borrow or buy a used crib, but be sure it meets these safety standards:

- The distance between the crib slats must be no more than 2⅜ inches. This is not only to keep baby's head from getting stuck; more important, this very small opening ensures that baby's wiggly body stays inside the crib.
- The inside must measure 27¼ inches by 51⅝ inches to fit a standard crib mattress. The Consumer Product Safety Commission gives this guideline: If you can fit more than two of your fingers between the

sides of the crib and the mattress, then the mattress is too small.

- The paint must be nontoxic, the hardware safe and all surfaces smooth.

- The movable side must be at least 26 inches higher than the mattress support at its lowest position to keep a child from climbing out easily.

- Some crib headboard and footboard designs may allow an infant's head to become caught in the openings between the finial (top of the bedpost) and the robe rail (horizontal piece along the top of the crib), or in other openings in the headboard structure. This may lead to strangulation. Look for a crib design either without the curved openings and bedposts or one where the opening is too large for the head to get caught. Many finials can be unscrewed and discarded.

☐ Don't move your child into his "big" bed right away. Use the bed mattress on the floor for a few days so he can get used to the change without being frightened of falling out.

☐ To start out, set the mattress and box springs on the floor next to the crib with the side down. When your child sleeps on the mattress, he'll have the bars of the crib on one side for security. Also, he can climb right into the crib if he *really* misses it.

☐ Put the bed in a corner and a guard rail on the side of the bed for criblike security. Or, put the bed against a wall, place the back of a dresser or bookcase at either end and a guard rail on the open side. The backs of the furniture can be decorated with posters, the child's artwork and so on.

☐ Use one side from the dismantled crib on the new bed to prevent falls. Just tie it onto the bed frame.

☐ Roll up two blankets and place them on either side of the bed under the bottom sheet. These "hills" make it hard to roll out of bed.

☐ Use the crib mattress next to the bed so that if the child falls out of bed, he lands on another mattress. Store the crib mattress under the bed during the day.

☐ On the night your child moves from crib to bed, give him a new stuffed animal or doll as a companion.

☐ Take pictures of your child on her first night in the big bed and it will make the evening very special. When the pictures are developed, hang a few over the bed.

Waking at Night

☐ One parent discovered that silence woke her daughter up: *"When my daughter turned two, she began to wake up just after we went to bed for no apparent reason. We finally realized that there was always a certain amount of noise in the house until we went to bed. After that, complete silence. So I put a radio near her room, turned it on low when I went to bed, and she slept contentedly every night thereafter."*

☐ If your child begins to wander into your room every night, try moving his bed to a different spot in the room. If he's in a crib, you might consider encouraging the switch to a regular bed. Sometimes a change in the child's environment will change his behavior.

☐ If you are trying to discourage visits to your bed at night, emphasize that she's welcome to come and snuggle in the *morning*. In other words, accentuate the positive.

☐ Explain that he's not to get up till it's light, and say good night with: "See you in the morning light!"

☐ Do not lock the door to your child's room, but do make sure all outside doors are locked.

☐ Lock the gates at the top of your stairs in case your child walks in his sleep.

☐ *"When our son was two and a half, he started to wake up in the middle of the night and come into our bed to sleep. For a while we let him, but then we tried to stop it. I got a lot of pressure from friends and family to stop it, too. We tried everything—gating his door, gating our door, rocking him to sleep, letting him cry—nothing worked. Finally my husband and I decided that he really must need to do this, so we gave up and let him come in. I was pregnant at the time and just had to get some sleep. Then, after the baby was born, she stayed in our room, so we couldn't justify keeping him out. But once we moved the baby out, he stopped waking up so much. Then I made a deal with him. I told him he could come into bed with me after his daddy left for work in the morning. This was our time while the baby was still asleep. And you know what? He started to wake up less and less. Now even when he gets up to go the bathroom at night, he goes back to his own bed."*

Night Fears

Night waking and fears often begin around age two and can continue into the threes. A frightened child who wakes at night must obviously be handled differently from the infant who woke up to play. Always discuss nightmares and bad dreams to try to get at what is scary and causing anxiety. My questionnaire query about night fears drew a tremendous response, indicating that this was a common problem, and yielded many useful ideas.

☐ Hang a picture of a guardian angel (or whatever would appeal to your child) near the bed. As one mother reports, *"I remember being comforted by such a picture as a child."* Family pictures are also helpful.

☐ Sew buttons on a soft cloth and explain that it's a "dream machine." If the child wakes up from a scary dream, he can just push one of the buttons for a better dream. Before bedtime discuss all the *nice* dreams he could have.

☐ Sing "My Favorite Things" from *The Sound of Music*. This works especially well if the child has seen the movie, but if not, you can tell the story of Maria and how she comforted frightened children during a thunderstorm by singing about her favorite things. "Whistle a Happy Tune" from *The King and I* is another good song to sing.

☐ Put a foldup bed in the child's room and tell her you will come and sleep there if she's scared in the night. *"This comforting thought helped my daughter sleep through the night."*

☐ Children are comforted when they learn they're not the only ones with night fears. Discuss what's happening with your child's nursery-school teachers; they may wish to talk about it in school. You can bet it's a common problem.

☐ Consider moving the child in temporarily with an older sibling, if the older one is willing. Waking up with company for a few nights is sometimes all it takes to quiet the night fears.

☐ Try superhero pajamas. Says one mother, *"My son sleeps in Superman pajamas, complete with red cape, red socks and red underpants over the pants. He has a lot of nightmares and this outfit seems to comfort him."*

☐ When the child is hysterical and you can't calm him with words or by holding him, lie down on his bed. Within a minute or two he will usually lie down next to you, and you can cuddle and talk. Usually the child is so exhausted by the hysteria that he'll fall right back to sleep.

☐ Night-lights that plug into wall sockets can create very frightening shadows. Try a 15-watt bulb in a lamp instead.

☐ Instead of night-lights, dim an overhead light. It's easy to install a dimmer switch yourself, and it gives you flexibility if you want to decrease the brightness gradually after the child has gone to sleep.

☐ A lighted fish tank is a good night-light as well as "company."

☐ Leave a flashlight near the bed. (The push-button kind works easily.)

☐ *"We finally gave up and left the room light on. Our electric bill is up, but he sleeps all night every night (well, almost)."*

What to Do About "Monsters"

Some parents are very opposed to going along with imaginary monsters, but acknowledging their existence in a light, humorous way and then dealing forcefully with them does seem to work most of the time to relieve the child's anxiety. Here are some ways to do that:

☐ Say some magic words, such as "abracadabra" or "shazoom," to make night creatures disappear for good.

☐ Be strong and courageous. Throw those monsters right out the window and lock it!

☐ Put a "magic" box on the child's dresser or windowsill. Fill it with potpourri (or anything scented) for a potent monster deterrent.

☐ *"For a 'man at the window' (on the second floor, no less), no amount of insisting would make my daughter believe that there was no one there, so we both told the man to go away—loudly—and he did!"*

☐ Say that the ghost (or whatever) is *also* asleep because it's nighttime and won't bother anyone.

☐ After reassuring the child ("I don't think there are any monsters, but let's look"), go around the room and look in the closet, under the bed and so on. Then command in a loud voice "Monsters, go away and don't come back!"

☐ A spray bottle filled with clear or colored water that you call "Monster-off" really gets rid of those monsters, especially if you and your child spray the room together. Don't forget under the bed and wherever else monsters often lurk!

☐ Walk around the outside of your house during the day and spray it with "Monster Spray."

9

Food

Food consumption varies a great deal in the toddler years. During a growth spurt toddlers seem to eat everything in sight; then, suddenly, they won't touch their favorite food. Forcing or bribing a child to eat is never a good idea. Mealtime should be a pleasurable experience, not a battleground. Always keep in mind that a child who is well and healthy will not starve himself. But there are times when some encouragement is a good idea. Here are ideas that may help:

Eating Encouragement

☐ Always have one food that she'll eat without fuss on her plate. Then she won't instantly reject her meal.

☐ Don't overload a child's plate. Small portions look more appetizing.

☐ A picky eater should have only nutritious snacks, such as fruit, cheese, vegetables, yogurt.

☐ Does your child beg for a snack right before dinner? Let him have a bit of whatever is on the dinner menu— nothing else.

☐ Put frozen peas in a cup for a delicious and healthful snack.

☐ Try serving food in its container (yogurt, canned vegetables, soup, etc.). Children sometimes eat far more this way than when it's plopped on a plate.

☐ *"My husband prefers snacks to meals. So does my son. It's a losing battle to get them to eat three good meals a day. So I keep healthful snacks on hand and have stopped worrying."*

☐ If your child refuses to try a new (or old) food, wait a day or so and serve it this way: Cut it into cubes and stick a toothpick in each. Then watch the food disappear.

☐ Grate raw carrots (and other raw vegetables) very finely and sneak them into tuna or egg salad.

☐ Try adding sautéed vegetables to omelettes for extra nutrition, but let your child choose what she wants from a selection of grated carrots, chopped broccoli, diced peppers, and the like.

☐ To get your child to finish all his milk, give him a cup with a picture printed on the bottom that can be seen only when all the liquid is gone. Or you can tape a picture to the bottom of a clear glass.

☐ A little vanilla, molasses or food coloring may entice a reluctant milk drinker. Let him stir. You could also drop something like a chocolate chip in his glass for him to eat when he has finished his milk.

☐ The milk goes down faster if you serve it with a colorful straw that bends.

☐ If you want to avoid the chocolate in chocolate milk, you can get a carob-drink mix in health-food stores that tastes just like it.

☐ If your child will not drink milk, put it into her food in powdered form. You can add powdered milk to all sorts of things—meat loaf, hamburgers, pancake mix, homemade bread—and don't forget melted cheese if she won't nibble plain cheese.

☐ Allergies to milk are fairly common and cause abdominal discomfort. If your child won't drink milk, do check with your doctor.

☐ When a toddler wouldn't eat the carrots in his stew, his grandmother told him, "I'm magic. I can make them disappear," and proceeded to mash them up with her fork. Now her grandchild says, "I'm magic, too." He mashes and eats.

☐ Cut sandwiches into letters or special shapes with cookie cutters. This makes the sandwich taste much better.

☐ Try smile sandwiches. Butter a piece of bread and let the child arrange cut-up cheese on it to resemble a smiling face. Broil until cheese melts.

☐ If you're seriously concerned that your child isn't eating enough, write down where he eats and when for a week or two. You may find that a late-afternoon snack kills his dinner appetite. Or that he nibbles enough fruit during the day to get all his vitamins.

☐ Your child might eat better if you served him his big meal at noon and a sandwich at suppertime.

☐ One mother reports, *"Sometimes there's an underlying reason for eating behavior that you must ferret out. My three-and-a-half-year-old almost stopped eating at one point. He finally told me the reason. He figured that if he didn't eat, he wouldn't grow; then he wouldn't get to be four and have to go to nursery school. Whew! That afternoon I took him to the nursery-school playground, and once he saw how much fun it was, he lost his fear and started eating."*

Mealtime

Don't expect a whole lot from twos. Meals should be pleasant (it's essential for digestion), and if your child can't cope yet with family meals, why agonize over it? Serve your child dinner before the family eats, and let him have his dessert while the rest of you are eating. Threes are generally more cooperative and can usually be included at mealtime.

☐ Constantly urging a child to take one more bite doesn't work in the long run. In fact, being pressured to eat really ruins the child's appetite as well as the appetite of others at the table. Give a child time to eat; then, if he starts playing rather than eating, take the food away.

☐ If dawdling and playing distract her from eating, set the timer for 5 or 10 minutes and tell her that if she hasn't finished her meal when the timer goes off, you will take away her plate and there will be no more food until the next meal.

☐ Always serve meals at the table (rather than snacking on the run) to encourage good manners and food habits.

☐ For variety at mealtime, serve your toddler's meals in an unusual container, such as a paper bag, plastic glasses or a toy truck.

☐ It's hard not to use dessert as a bribe for finishing a meal, but dessert should not be viewed as a reward. However, it should be made clear, as one mother does to her child, that "If you're not hungry enough to finish dinner, you aren't hungry enough for dessert."

☐ Don't make a habit of serving dessert with every meal. Then the child won't be as likely to "save room" for it.

☐ If your child is cranky at mealtime, try feeding her earlier. She may just be too hungry to be pleasant.

☐ *"Sometimes we hunt for our lunch and find it in a bag hanging on a tree or in a closet. It tastes better after the thrill of the chase."*

☐ Pay attention to between-meal snacks. A small but constant supply of food and/or juice can easily kill appetites at mealtime.

☐ Be flexible with eating hours. A child might not always be hungry exactly at noon. Interrupting a favorite activity can also make the child less interested in eating.

☐ Don't insist that everything be finished, but do insist that everything be tried.

☐ Expect your child to finish dinner and dessert before you've finished your first course. Then excuse him and finish your dinner in peace.

☐ Don't be too fussy about manners at this age, unless your child is deliberately provoking you. With gentle reminders and realistic expectations—plus exemplary manners on your part—your child *will* eventually have good table manners.

☐ If you want your child to enjoy a particular type of music, play it during mealtime. He will always associate it with something pleasant and will like it for the rest of his life.

Cooking with Children's Help

Kitchen projects require great patience on your part, but the look of satisfaction on your child's face as he eats his very own cooking will be worth it. Begin only when you're *both* rested and in good moods. Be sensitive to your child's interests; a two-year-old's approach to cooking will be very different from your own. As one mother put it: *"I discovered that I get very compulsive about achieving perfection when making cookies with a cookie cutter. All my fantasies of harmonious mother-daughter baking disappear when Jessica cannot cut cookies properly. After trying many ways to get her to do it my way, it finally occurred to me that she can't do it otherwise, nor does she care.*

"The successful solution that resulted in fun for us both was to give Jess her own rolling pin (a plastic rod from some blocks), her own small mound of dough, her own cookie cutters and sheets. She happily cuts out small semismashed bits and places them in her pan while I am able to make my own perfect cookies. We then put both cookie sheets in the oven. She is delighted to have her own cookies to offer to her father and me."

General Observations

☐ A two may suddenly develop bizarre food likes and dislikes. Refusals to eat "lumpy" foods, gravy or anything green are common. Don't fight it; it's a part of a general negative stage. There are plenty of nutritious foods you can substitute, and the stage will not last forever.

☐ If your child won't eat the heels of the bread loaf, make the sandwich so that the brown outside is *inside* the sandwich and he'll never know it's the heel.

☐ The heavy plastic yogurt containers make great cups. Save the lids and you can easily store leftover juice or milk in the refrigerator.

☐ Serve soup in an oversize coffee cup or mug. Little ones like to hold on to the handle while they spoon it up, and toward the end they can pick it up to get the last drops.

☐ If bibs are being resisted, try a big cowboy bandanna instead.

☐ *"When I was lunching at a friend's house, I knew she was doing something right when her children jumped up and down with delight as she brought on the first course: broccoli. She cooked it perfectly, so it was still crunchy, but the real secret is, she serves it as a first course, when the children are good and hungry."* A similar idea: If your child is ravenous for a snack right before dinner, let him eat the vegetable course.

☐ Make an "eating out" box to keep in your car. Fill it with a clean bib, plastic cup, small toys, crayons—and *only* use it at restaurants.

☐ Meat loaf and hamburgers can disguise all sorts of added nutritious ingredients, such as powdered milk, pureed vegetables, wheat germ, and the like.

☐ Whenever you can add fruit juice or broth to a dish rather than water, do so.

☐ Try applesauce (and/or other mashed fruit) instead of jelly on peanut-butter sandwiches.

☐ Don't let your child lick peanut butter from his finger or a spoon. Too big a glob could stick in his throat.

☐ If your child loves apples but constantly drops them, try this: Core the apple. String ribbon or yarn through the hole and tie it around the child's neck like a necklace. But keep your eye on him whenever he has something around his neck.

☐ Put slices of apples or other cut-up fruit in a paper cup so that your child can carry them around easily.

☐ For a portable meal, serve tuna, ham or egg salad in an ice-cream cone.

☐ Children often go on food jags when they'll only eat one or two foods. As long as the foods are relatively nutritious (peanut butter, for example), don't worry about it. The stage will pass more quickly if you don't fuss.

☐ Many children have adverse reactions to foods containing artificial additives and preservatives and too much sugar. Avoid these whenever possible. If your child's behavior seems more erratic than it should be, consult your doctor. Allergies and/or special sensitivities may be the problem.

☐ Avoid any food product containing caffeine, a stimulant your child does not need.

10

Working and Parenting

When both parents work outside the home, life can get extremely complicated. The demands on your time and energy will probably never be greater than when your child is in the toddler years. Is it worth it? It can be, but don't fool yourself. It takes flexibility, organization, resilience and a lot of hard work!

Child Care

DAY-CARE CENTERS

☐ Call your state's Department of Social Services, Health or Human Resources to check on the licensing requirements for day-care centers.

☐ If you choose to send your child to a day-care center, you will want to know the answers to these questions:

- Will the same people take care of your child most of the time, or will personnel change constantly?
- What are the qualifications of the staff?
- Do the caregivers seem to genuinely love children?
- Do the children seem to be happy? Well behaved?

- How many children will be under each caregiver's supervision? Does each child receive individual attention during the day?
- What is the daily schedule? Are special activities ever planned?
- What kind of activities (such as art, water play, cooking, science) are available to the children? Will your child have plenty of physical activity as well as adequate rest? Will there be opportunities for creative play and interaction with adults? Can children sometimes choose their own activities?
- Do they keep a record of your child's activities and meet with you on a regular basis?
- Are there enough toys and play equipment, and are they in good condition? Is the playground safe? (See "Outdoors," pages 61–62.)
- Are the meals and snacks nutritious?
- What is their policy in case the child is ill or injured?
- How do they discipline children?
- What is the general atmosphere of the center? Is it homey and cheerful or large and institutional? Would you want to spend an entire day there?
- Will they give you names and phone numbers of other parents using the center?
- How do they deal with a child who bites? How do they take care of a bitten child?

☐ Try to contact parents of children who attend the same day-care center. If problems come up, they will be solved more easily if they are shared. And you may be able to work out a co-op transportation plan.

☐ Stay in constant touch with day-care personnel to find out how your child is doing, what she is eating, when she is sleeping and so on. It's so easy to fall into the habit of letting others take over completely.

☐ Take your child's blankets from home to the child care center. The familiar fragrance and feel will comfort children away from home.

☐ If you send lunch, do check occasionally to see if your child is eating it. *"I learned, to my dismay, that the yogurt I sent was never touched,"* said one mother. *"My child's teacher always meant to tell me but would forget by the time 5 P.M. rolled around."*

☐ Ask to see weekly menus. Check on what your child is eating there so you can encourage expanded tastes. If there are eating problems, work closely with the center as a partner on solutions.

☐ Identify toys, lunch boxes and the like with a small picture of your child for easy recognition by nonreaders.

☐ Put a loving note and small treats in your child's lunch box occasionally.

☐ You can arrange for the nursery-school bus to drop your child off at the day-care center.

☐ It helps if one parent takes the child to the center or sitter and the other parent picks them up.

☐ Check your library or bookstore for books you can read to your child about day care and parents who work outside the home.

FOR MORE INFORMATION

☐ Contact the National Association for Child Care Resource and Referral Agencies for names of organizations in your area that can help you with child care options and decisions. Write to NACCRRA, 2116 Campus Drive SE, Rochester, MN 55904, or call (507) 287-2220.

☐ To obtain the free brochure "Finding the Best Care for Infant or Toddler," send a self-addressed, stamped envelope to the National Association for the Education of Young Children, Box HC, 1834 Connecticut Ave. N.W., Washington, D.C. 20009.

FAMILY DAY-CARE PROVIDERS

☐ To locate a person who sits for children in her home, try:
   • Advertising, not only in the local paper but with signs at supermarkets, community centers and the like.
   • Recommendations from preschools and nursery schools.
   • A senior citizen center.
   • Local colleges.
   • Churches and synagogues.
   • Telling everyone you know—and even people you don't know (such as shopkeepers)—that you're looking for someone. Good recommendations can come from unexpected sources.
   • The local branch of your state's Department of Labor or Social Services. Find out if child care in private homes is licensed or regulated, and if so, what the requirements are. They may be able to provide you with a list of licensed homes.

- The National Association for Child Care Resource and Referral Agencies at (507) 287-2220. They can recommend an agency in your local area.

☐ Day-care centers and licensed family day-care providers must meet certain standards, but you are responsible for checking out unregulated day-care providers. Look over the checklist for day-care centers; you will want similar information on any caregiver you are considering. In addition, ask:

- Is the home safe? Is the outdoor play equipment safe? What safety rules are enforced?
- Will the caregiver ever have to transport your child in her car? Are car seats available and used?
- Does the caregiver have any medical problems?
- If the caregiver is sick or becomes ill suddenly (one sitter had a serious allergic reaction to a bee sting), does she have backup support close by?
- Are your basic principles of child care compatible with the caregiver's?

☐ If the sitter has a child very close to your child's age, be aware that the other child may be very jealous. Although it's nice for your child to have a companion, it often works out better if your child is younger or older than the child who lives in the house.

☐ Every once in a while give the sitter paper and new crayons to be brought out at afternoon snack time. Have her ask the child to draw what he did that day so he can share it with Mom and Dad.

☐ Be clear with the child care provider about naps. If a long nap keeps you and your child up too late, ask the provider to shorten afternoon sleep. On weekends, try to keep the work-week schedule going. This makes life easier and more consistent for your child.

☐ Make sure to fill your caregiver in on the schedules and routines that help your child settle down to sleep.

☐ Spend time talking to the person caring for your child so you can explain your child's eating schedule, likes and dislikes. You and the caregiver need to be in partnership with each other; listen to her good ideas, too.

☐ Your sitter should have your child's complete medical history and immunization chart. Fill out the charts on pages 233–234 and give her a copy.

☐ Always leave a notarized authorization slip with your sitter, giving her permission to authorize emergency medical treatment for your child if you cannot be reached. Check with your local hospital to see if they have a consent form. If not, use this sample form:

MEDICAL EMERGENCY CONSENT FORM

From _____ to _____
                (date)   (date)
_____ has my permission to authorize
            (caregiver)

for _____
                    (child or children's names)
any emergency medical treatment in my absence.

Our pediatrician is _____ at _____
                            (name)   (phone)

_____
                          (address)
Allergies/Special Conditions _____

_____

Insurance Company _____

Policy or Benefit Code Numbers _____

                          Signed (both parents if possible)

_____   _____
          (date)

                          _____

The parent/legal guardian named above agrees to hold harm-
less the person appointed and the physician providing treatment from and against any and all loss, costs, damage, or
expense of any kind arising out of or in connection with that
person's or physician's acting in reliance upon the authorization set forth herein, with the exception of actions which
amount to gross negligence. The physician shall not be re-
lieved on the basis of this authorization from liability for
negligence in the diagnosis and treatment of a minor.

☐ When your child is mastering new skills, such as toilet training or self-dressing, make sure your sitter knows what you're doing at home. Your child will learn more quickly when all the adults who care for him are insisting on the same actions and procedures.

☐ Take advantage of your baby-sitter to introduce or reinforce new skills. Sometimes the child will accept direction from the sitter when he resists you.

☐ Remember that children are very adaptable and can conform to different rules in different homes without any detrimental effect.

☐ Be sure to let caregivers know of any important events that took place at home (accidents, visit from grandparents, birthdays).

☐ Keep a notebook in your child's diaper bag. In the notebook, write down all the schedules, needs, desires and habits of your child. Then use it to send notes (and thank yous) to the sitter; the sitter can write in things you need to know as they occur. This notebook is especially helpful for new or emergency sitters.

☐ Give your child's substitute mom praise and support when she's doing a good job.

IN-HOME PROVIDERS

Please read the previous sections for tips that also apply to in-home care. In addition:

☐ To locate a person to care for your children in your own home, check the family day-care provider list on pages 150–151. You can also call:

- Employment agencies. Many specialize in child care providers. Check with your state's Department of Labor to see if they are licensed or regulated and what the requirements are. Do not assume that just because they are licensed, they will meet your hiring standards. For example, in New York, agencies are required by law to check only one reference; you should demand more checks.
- The International Nanny Association at (512) 454-6462 for information about hiring nannies.

☐ Screen candidates over the phone. If you want to find out more about them without committing yourself, say "I'm seeing someone today, but why don't you tell me about yourself, and if this person doesn't work out, I'll call you back."

☐ Determine what you should (and can afford to) pay by checking rates with friends and employment agencies.

☐ Check and double check all references given to you by the person you've chosen to care for your child, even if the person has been referred by an agency. Be extra careful.

☐ Check the person's driving record before you hire. Call your Motor Vehicle Bureau to find out how to do this in your area.

☐ Keep the relationship as professional as possible. Set specific working hours. Allow for ample time off. Encourage participation in nanny workshops and peer group discussions.

☐ Be strict and very careful at the beginning of your relationship. You can always ease up later once you get to know one another.

☐ Pay for a CPR course for your caregiver.

☐ Keep the lines of communication open. Set a time each week to discuss any problems. Write them down as they occur, and resolve them.

☐ It is extremely important that your caregiver has a life of her own and does not feel lonely. If your nanny lives in and does not know anyone but you in the area, encourage socializing by:

- Calling other nannies in the area and inviting them over for a few pizza parties.
- Signing up your baby and nanny for programs at the library, community center or elsewhere.
- Asking mothers of older children what parks in your area would be good places for your sitter to meet other sitters.
- Providing her with her own phone line.

☐ There's a lot of stress involved in caring for children. Some families provide health club memberships for their caregivers.

☐ Go home for surprise visits every once in a while.

☐ Keep the same routines your baby enjoys. Write them down in detail for the sitter.

☐ Fill out the medical emergency consent form on page 153 and give it to your sitter.

Getting Out/Coming Back

☐ Have the child's clothes ready the night before—that means coats, hats, mittens, boots and lunch boxes, too. If he's fussy about his outfits, have him select them then so there is no arguing in the morning.

☐ Allowing more time for everything, especially in the morning, is essential.

☐ It's vital to get the children to bed early. As one parent put it, *"Letting them stay up to see a special TV program was no favor for anyone the next day."*

☐ Discuss transition times with your child care provider so that you both know what to expect and can support each other. Decide on the routine that will make your child feel the most comfortable.

☐ Familiar routines can ease farewells, such as a kiss through the window or a promise to call when you get to work.

☐ *Never* sneak out. Doing so only confirms the child's feeling of distrust in the situation.

☐ A parent reports, *"Although I'm opposed to TV cartoons, we now watch one program during breakfast. I've discovered that my daughter eats a better breakfast if we do more than stare at each other. It also helps to set time limits. She understands we have to leave when the program is over and is cooperative, whereas I never got anywhere with 'It's eight o'clock, let's go.' Also she gets dressed promptly because she must be dressed before the TV goes on."*

☐ Your child will look forward to the ride to the babysitter's if you have landmarks of interest along the way, such as "How many bulldozers will we find at the construction site today?" or "Will there be any children on the swings in the park today?"

☐ Stagger your schedules. Mom and Dad should each have time alone with the child at opposite ends of the day.

☐ Always take the time to be with your child and play when you *first* get home. Dinner can wait. Then, if you really need a bit of privacy, go to the bathroom.

☐ The end of the day is hard for everybody. Create a time— even five minutes—for consciously making the transition from work to home. One mother told me she gives her toddler all the junk mail and a safe letter opener. While she reads the mail, her little one is absorbed in "his" mail.

☐ Count on a lot of acting out once you get home after work. It's been saved up all day with the sitter. Testing, anger and other guilt-inducing behavior is developmentally normal and occurs with all children, not only those of working parents.

☐ If you have to drive a long way to work, consider leaving the child with a sitter near your job rather than near your home. You get more time with him this way during the rides to and from work.

Working at Home

☐ If you're buying a phone-answering machine, get one that has a call-in feature. That way if you're out for the day, you can call in to find out if there is any message from your sitter about an emergency or problem.

☐ Allow your child to be part of your work. Toddlers can stick on stamps, take copies from a copying machine, gather loose paper clips and so on.

☐ For days when there's no sitter and you have to work:

- Provide the child with the tools of your trade (toy typewriter, telephone, erasers, etc.) so he can imitate you and, more important, so that he won't demand your things.
- Have special toys in your office that she can play with provided she's quiet.
- You will have to devote some exclusive time to your child. Just explain that after a certain amount of time, he will have to play by himself. Set a timer; when it goes off, it will be play time again, but not before!
- Call a friend who doesn't work or has a different schedule and invite her and her child over. Explain that you need working time, and she'll probably welcome the distraction and be happy to help. Don't forget to return the favor.
- If your work is portable, take the child to a playground and work on a park bench.

☐ When you get an important business call, try these:

- Keep an extra purse near the phone filled with safe things the child can discover and play with.
- Allow sink play within your view with soapy water and plastic utensils.

- Use food as a distraction. *"My two-year-old son was in the high chair for breakfast when an important business call came for me. I gave him a box of cereal and had a long, peaceful conversation. Of course, there was cereal all over the place when I got back to him, but he'd been happy and quiet—what more could I ask?"*
- Keep some masking tape near the phone. Stick some on her to pull off. Tangle it for her to untangle.

General Observations

☐ Check into the possibility of working flexible hours at your company. An 11 A.M.–to–7 P.M. schedule may suit your family better than 9 to 5.

☐ You may be able to work fewer hours but keep your job by sharing it with someone and only working part time.

☐ Plan to do most of your cooking on weekends and freeze a lot, so that when you come home you can spend time with your child rather than cooking. Freeze food in portions. You'll then be able to heat her dinner quickly if she's really hungry.

☐ Hire a baby-sitter on Saturday so you can do all your errands quickly. Then you'll have more exclusive time to devote to your child.

☐ Even a three-year-old can do certain household chores. Simple accomplishments such as setting the table, filling the laundry basket or sorting socks will be a source of pride to your child and may free your hands for other things.

☐ Clean and save your medicine bottles with the childproof caps. Then when your child needs noontime medication away from home, measure out five days' worth (or whatever) into the bottle for your sitter to keep. Carefully relabel the bottle with child's and medication's names, current dosage, and any refrigeration requirements. This saves having to deliver and pick up the medicine every day. In most states, child care providers in centers or homes are required to have a doctor's note to authorize their giving any medication.

☐ If you have the kind of job that has deadlines, try to avoid a winter deadline. Twos and threes get every type of flu and cold known, and so, occasionally, do sitters.

☐ At your office, leave a note by your phone giving your location whenever you leave your desk, even for lunch. You never know when that emergency call from your child's caregiver is going to come in.

☐ Each parent should find an opportunity to bring the child to work, so he has a good picture of where his parents go after dropping him off. It's a real treat for the child.

☐ Bring your child's artwork to the office, framed for display. Be sure to tell her that so-and-so from the office likes her picture.

☐ Contact other parents in your business or industry to find out what problems they share and which solutions work best.

FOR MORE INFORMATION

☐ Contact the National Association for Child Care Resource and Referral Agencies for organizations in your area that can help you with child care options and decisions.

Write: NACCRRA, 2116 Campus Drive SE, Rochester, MN 55904, or call (507) 287-2220.

☐ Parents interested in hiring a nanny can get more information from the International Nanny Association, P.O. Box 26522, Austin, TX 78755 (512) 454-6462.

☐ National Association for Family Day Care will help you find accredited day care in your area. Write: NAFDC, 725 15th Street, NW, Suite 505, Washington, D.C. 20005, or call (202) 347-3356.

☐ These newsletters may be helpful:

"Welcome Home" (monthly) by Mothers At Home. For subscription information, call (800) 783-4MOM or write: Mothers at Home, 8310A, Old Courthouse Road, Vienna, VA 22182.

"Homeworking Mothers" (quarterly) by Mothers' Home Business Network. For subscription information, call (516) 997-7394 or write: Mothers' Home Business Network, P.O. Box 423, East Meadow, NY 11554.

Home Based Business Newspaper (quarterly) by the National Association of Home Based Businesses, Inc. For subscription information, call (410) 363-3698 or write: NAHBB, P.O. Box 30220, Baltimore, MD 21270.

11

Traveling

The response most often given to the question "How do you keep your toddler content while traveling?" was "Take along a battery-operated cassette player with cassettes of the child's favorite songs and stories." Don't forget the headphones!

By Car

☐ Find a box that fits under the seat and keep little toys, books, crayons, papers and the like in it. The box top can be used as a desk.

☐ When your toddler is alone in the backseat and there is another adult with you, take turns sitting in the back with her. The company and change of companion may keep her from getting too restless.

☐ Small cloth puppets or flashcards can be stored easily in the glove compartment. A front-seat passenger can use them to entertain a backseat audience.

☐ Frequent stops are important. Active toddlers need to run around every two hours or so.

☐ Don't give the child anything to drink in the car during the trip. It will only lead to more potty stops, and what a mess if it spills. Take only water if you must have something.

☐ A runner's water bottle is great for thirsty toddlers on car trips.

☐ Use a sand pail for roadside potty stops.

☐ If you rent a car, find out in advance if the rental company will supply or rent you a car seat. Many do not, and those that do may run out of them by the time you arrive, especially during holidays and other peak traveling times. To be absolutely safe, you may wish to take your own seat.

CAR SEATS AND SAFETY

Answers to the most frequently asked questions about car seats are given below. This information was supplied by the Westchester County Traffic Safety Board.

Why are child-restraint seats needed?

- Automobile accidents are the leading cause of death and injury to children.
- Regular seat belts are not desirable for children under the age of four or for children less than 40 pounds and 40 inches because of their delicate body and bone structure.
- A 10-pound infant will be thrown forward with a

force of 300 pounds during an impact if a car is traveling at 30 miles per hour. That's like falling from a three-story building. There is no way an adult can hold back a 300-pound force. If the adult is holding a child but not wearing a seat belt, the adult's body will crush the child upon impact.

- Restraint systems hold a child in the car and safely spread the forces of the crash over a wide body area.
- They instill the habit of always using a restraint system.
- Children must be buckled up. It's the law.

Important considerations to keep in mind when selecting a restraint seat:

- The "best" restraint seat is the one in which your child will be most comfortable, that you can anchor properly in your car(s) and that you are willing to use *every* time you travel.
- If a restraint seat has a top anchor strap, it must be fastened to a special anchor plate installed in the rear or to a set of rear lap belts. It must be pulled *tight*. If you cannot or are not willing to do this, buy a restraint seat that is anchored only by a lap belt.
- The restraint seat must be properly used. The manufacturer's instructions *must* be followed for the device to give proper protection. Correct installation is essential!
- Check to see if the car seat you're buying has undergone "dynamic testing," which means it has been tested under crash conditions. Do not buy an old car seat—certainly not one made before 1981. Car seats

manufactured after January 1, 1981, must meet federal standards (FMVSS 213), which require dynamic testing.

- Some restraint seats cannot be used in certain model vehicles or in certain seating positions. See if the restraint will fit where you want to use it in your car before you buy it. The lap belt should fit around it and adjust *snugly*.

- Make sure the restraint seat elevates your child enough to see out the window. It is particularly important that children prone to car sickness are able to see out of the car easily.

- Check your car's owner's manual for any information on restraint seat use.

If your child must ride in a car that does not have a car seat, use the regular seat belt. The belt should fit snugly over the hip/thigh bones.

TIPS FROM PARENTS

☐ Push the seat back and forth to test for tightness. If it moves, tighten it.

☐ Don't start the car until everyone is buckled up, adults included. How can you ask children to buckle if you don't do it yourself?

☐ If anyone unbuckles his seat belt while you're driving, just pull over to the side of the road and explain that you're not moving till it's buckled again. Don't say another word. The silent treatment works much better than yelling or nagging.

☐ You will find it's much easier to drive when your children are buckled up. There's no more horsing around, poking, hanging out the window and all those other things that drive you crazy.

☐ In summer the metal parts on car seats can get hot enough to burn a child. To prevent this, cover the whole car seat with a large towel (or anything else) every time you leave the car. It's not a bad idea to cover your own seat, too.

☐ *"I'm an X-ray technician and have seen too many children die because they weren't in car seats. We made it a week's project of our mothers' group to check out prices, types of seats and safety features of each in all our local stores. That way we saved time, money and everybody learned something."*

☐ Always fill out and send in the registration card for the car seat. You'll then receive any information on recalls.

☐ READ THE DIRECTIONS! Car seats are not safe unless they are used according to the manufacturer's directions.

☐ See pages 60–61 for more information on car safety.

FIVE GOOD RULES TO ENFORCE

- Always buckle up.
- No yelling.
- No hitting, biting and the like.
- Never touch door handles.
- Never play in the car alone.

FOR MORE INFORMATION

☐ To find out about car seats or local car seat loan programs, contact the Governor's Traffic Safety Committee in your state.

☐ Send a business-size, self-addressed, stamped envelope to "Family Shopping Guide," American Academy of Pediatrics, P.O. Box 927, Elk Grove, IL 60009-0927. Take along this guide when you're shopping for seats; it lists all safe models and their features.

☐ For more information on helping your child enjoy riding in a car seat or transporting children with special needs, send a self-addressed, stamped envelope to Safe Ride Program, American Academy of Pediatrics, 141 Northwest Point Boulevard, P.O. Box 927, Elk Grove Village, IL 60009-0927.

☐ If you have a car seat problem or a question, call the manufacturer directly. Many have toll-free numbers. Call (800) 555-1212 for the toll-free phone number information. Any problem should also be reported to the National Highway Traffic Safety Administration (see below).

☐ The National Highway Traffic Safety Administration has a hotline for car-seat recalls and safety tips: (800) 424-9393 (in Washington, D.C., call 366-0123).

By Airplane

☐ When traveling, label your child with *his* name, *your* name and any pertinent information, such as "Flying with (name of airline)." If you get separated, this will speed your reunion. Also stick the label *inside* his clothes, so he doesn't pick it off!

☐ If you have to change planes, check with your airline to see if they allow you to bring a stroller on board. If you have to make your way through a large airport, a stroller can be a lifesaver.

☐ Consider a harness and leash if you must change planes. If the child is used to walking with you this way, she can get some good exercise in the airport, and you won't have to worry about losing her.

☐ Take a small ball or football to play with at the airport. It encourages activity and attracts playmates.

☐ Give children their own flight bag or small backpack to take on plane trips. It can be filled with special toys and other amusements of their choice. Of course, it mustn't be so heavy or bulky that you end up carrying it.

☐ A cosmetic bag with many zippered pockets filled with various goodies can entertain a child for a long time. The zippers alone will do it.

☐ Car seats can be used on a plane only if they have been safety tested for this use. If the seat is approved for airline use, it will carry a sticker stating so.

☐ Use a backpack to carry all your traveling essentials: diapers, bottles, food, even your purse.

☐ Many airlines have special children's meals available, but be sure to check this with the airline and order ahead if necessary.

☐ Take something for the child to chew or suck (sugarless gum, a bottle) during takeoff and landing to relieve ear pressure.

☐ A word of warning: *"Don't count too much on food to occupy your toddler on a plane. Mine ate from New York to Denver and lost it all over both of us during the landing!"*

☐ If there is the remotest chance your child might have an ear infection, ask your doctor for a prescription to keep the ear canals open.

☐ For a very long plane ride, your doctor may recommend some kind of medication for nausea. Check this with the doctor.

☐ Most airlines will allow you and your child to visit the cockpit and pilots after the plane has landed. Ask about a visit. Use it to reinforce traveling rules. ("See, the pilots wear their seat belts, too.")

15 Activities for Traveling Tots

- A cassette player with cassettes of favorite stories or songs. Use earphones if your child doesn't object, but check the volume yourself before she puts them on.
- A book of cutouts, old magazines or toy catalogs and scissors. You can find punch-out books, too; scissors aren't needed.
- Paper dolls with clothes.
- Electronic games.
- Pipe cleaners.
- Coloring books, anticoloring books, pad of paper, crayons.
- Paint books that require water only.
- Pressure-sensitive dots, stars and other shapes.
- Murals with vinyl stick-on animals and characters.
- New paperback storybooks about planes, buses, boats, trains—however you're traveling.
- Wind-up toys that make sounds or music boxes.
- Coins for counting, sorting, stacking.

- Simple, light models of planes, dinosaurs and the like to build with Mom or Dad.
- Game books with mazes, hidden pictures or whatever.
- Bubble solution.

Moving

BEFORE THE MOVE

☐ Reports one mother, *"I remember overhearing my parents talk about moving long before they discussed it with me. I was so frightened, confused and unhappy."* Be sure your children don't go through this; discuss the move (even a possible move) as soon as you can.

☐ Moving is an overwhelming experience for you, but it's even more so for your children. Even though you're very busy, try to spend extra time with them during this period. Doing so will really pay off by making the move a happier one.

☐ Sometimes a child's confusion can be well disguised. One mother was moving from a house to an apartment, and she and her two-and-a-half-year-old son discussed the move and the apartment often. But when he was asked by a friend what an apartment was, he answered, "a toy."

☐ Storybooks about moving can make the concept of moving clearer to your child and help relieve anxieties. Ask your local librarian or bookstore for suggestions.

☐ Take the child to the new home often, if possible. If not, draw or show pictures of it. Talk about all the good things your child will find there (a playroom, a bigger yard, etc.).

☐ Don't forget to take pictures of the local parks, playgrounds and other places of interest to children in the new locality. If you can take pictures of neighborhood children, even better!

☐ Your child will need to be reassured often that pets, toys and furniture will all go with you.

☐ Play moving games:

- Build the new house out of blocks. Talk about each room as you build.
- Playact Moving Day with little play people. Use trucks to move furniture. Set up the old residence in one room, then "move" to another.
- Use a dollhouse for fantasy play. You might want to move in and out of it several times before your real move. On the day of the move, your child can put the furniture into a special box. Then, when you get to your destination, he can unpack and settle in, just as you're doing.

☐ Do discuss decorating the child's new bedroom and find out if she wants it to be exactly the same as it was or if she wants to try something new.

☐ Take *all* the child's toys and things to the new home. This is not the time to sort out the junky stuff. He'll feel much better if he sees *everything* being packed.

☐ Each day as you pack, have your little one pack a box for himself, so he is reassured that he is moving, too.

☐ Buy something special (lamp, sheets, posters, radio) for the child's room in the new house. Don't let it be used until move-in day!

☐ If your child has just made the transition from crib to bed, he might need the security of the crib again during or after the move, so have it available.

☐ Send a welcome card or letter to your child, sign it with his friends' names, and mail it so it will arrive when you're moving in.

☐ Be sure movers put the child's boxes and furniture on *last*, and mark them UNLOAD FIRST.

☐ On moving day settle the children in first. Unpacking their own toys will probably be a treat for them while you unpack the clothes.

AFTER THE MOVE

☐ Don't be surprised if babyish behavior reappears. Regression at this time is common. Be patient; moves can be very tough for preschoolers.

☐ Spend a lot of time in the child's new room at the beginning.

☐ Plan at least one activity a day that will be fun for you and your children, such as discovering the library, visiting the local ice cream parlor and so on.

☐ A phone call or two to some dear friends might make your child feel better.

☐ Don't forget that leisurely walks are the best way to explore your new neighborhood. And it's the way to meet neighbors and children.

☐ Pretend you and your child are explorers each time you go out. Even a trip to the dry cleaner can be made into a big adventure.

☐ When you visit the new supermarket, ask your toddler to help you find things in the new place. She'll be so proud of herself as she tells you where familiar food items are.

Vacations

WITH THE CHILDREN

☐ Don't forget

- night-light
- flannel-covered rubber sheet or plastic mattress cover
- child's own sheets, blanket, pillow, sleeping toys and so on
- any prescription medicine you might need for runny noses and other ailments
- first-aid kit
- medicine spoons
- diapers and rubber pants in case regression occurs
- portable cassette player with many song and story cassettes
- electric outlet covers

☐ If you must leave *very* early on a trip, let your child wear her "trip" clothes to bed so you won't have to dress a grumpy toddler in the morning.

☐ If you're renting a cottage, ask your landlord to help with whatever you need. One mother said that such a request turned up a playpen and two reliable baby-sitters.

☐ Don't lug a lot of equipment along with you when you travel. Many towns have rental services from which you can get cribs, high chairs, strollers and other equipment.

☐ Resort and hotel brochures do get out of date. Before you choose your spot, make sure that all the children's facilities they promise are still there.

☐ Be sure the resort *really* caters to and welcomes children. A phone call to the manager is a good investment.

☐ Many theme/amusement parks rent strollers. Check this out.

☐ Don't try to cram too many activities into each day. Plan for less, and if you're able to do more (if the child isn't tired and cranky), it will be a pleasant surprise.

☐ Rest periods help *everyone* in midafternoon.

☐ Don't forget to send postcards to your child's friends. They'll be delighted, and with any luck their parents will remember to send your child mail when they go away.

☐ The last word: *"No matter where you go, bring favorite toys, coloring books, crayons, raisins, peanut butter and jelly. Nothing else matters!"*

WITHOUT THE CHILD

☐ Talk to your pediatrician before you leave about the possibility of emergencies. Will he/she take the responsibility for ordering emergency treatment? Will a near relative have to be called in case you can't be reached? Pediatricians appreciate this courtesy, and it will certainly help you relax.

☐ Plan your children's time yourself; don't leave it all up to the sitter. Invite friends over, plan beach trips, what have you. Leave one gift for a rainy day, and give one gift just before leaving so they have something to do just after you leave.

☐ Before you go, write each child a letter for each day you'll be gone. Address it, put it in an envelope and have your sitter give each child his "mail" every day, as if it came in the mail.

☐ Sometimes talking to the child on the phone makes her very upset. Threes seem to cope better with phone calls than twos, but you know your child. It's sometimes better if the sitter holds the phone near the child so you can hear her happily playing.

☐ Make some tape recordings for your toddler. Tell funny stories, jokes, read stories.

☐ Allow yourself a half hour per day to talk about your child—that's all!

12

Toys, Games and Amusements

Toys and Games

☐ Two- and three-year-olds will enjoy toys that allow them to imitate adults: wheelbarrow, broom, typewriter, and the like.

☐ Consider buying very sturdy doll cradles and high chairs, because children will often try to use them themselves.

☐ Number each piece from a puzzle on the back with the same number. (Puzzle #1 has *1* on the back of each piece.) If they get mixed up, you can sort them out easily. You can also assign a color to each puzzle and put a dot of that color on the back of each piece to identify it.

☐ When buying puzzles for small children, avoid the thin cardboard kind. The pieces are difficult for children to work with, and the picture often separates from the cardboard piece. They also warp.

☐ Pipe cleaners are good "church toys." They're quiet, safe and you can carry them in your purse.

☐ A two-year-old is easily frustrated by toys that are not easy to work. For instance, the hook-and-eye attachments on some toy trains are hard to manipulate. Trains that attach with magnets are better buys.

☐ Many interlocking-type toys are too hard for most twos and threes, but they're great to have around for adults and teenage baby-sitters to play with. The child enjoys "helping," the adult enjoys building and they both have fun.

☐ Small rollers made for painting trim are fabulous toys. You can buy them at any hardware store. Just give children a bucket of water and rollers and let them "paint" the sidewalk (porch, deck, etc.) to their heart's content. Wide paintbrushes also work well, but there's something special about a roller.

☐ Two-year-olds are often fascinated by any toy with moving parts or gears that they can watch.

☐ Save and store the original boxes that good toys come in. Then, when your child has outgrown them, they can be cleaned and put back in their own box, ready to pass on to the next sibling as gifts, and they'll look brand new.

☐ Keep your eyes open for discarded cardboard boxes, especially those that new refrigerators, washing machines and stoves come in. Giant boxes have limitless uses. They can be a house one day and a boat the next.

☐ Recycle plastic bottles as bath or beach toys. The "squirt" kind (such as old shampoo bottles, syrup containers) are the most fun. Be sure they are *thoroughly* clean. Do not use bottles that held cleaners or other strong chemicals.

☐ Coat paper decals on toys with clear nail polish. The toy will be easier to keep clean and it will look fresher longer.

☐ For an outdoor sandbox, punch holes in a plastic wading pool and fill it with coarse builders' sand. Be sure to locate the sandbox where there is shade, especially in the afternoon. Cover it so pets don't use it as a litter box.

☐ A three- to four-foot plastic pool slide can be used all year round.

☐ On a slip of paper that fits into your wallet, make a list of all your child's toys that require batteries. Note battery type and size.

Toy Safety

☐ Select toys to suit the age, skills, abilities and interests of the child. Look for labels that give age-appropriate recommendations, and heed them.

☐ Look for sturdy construction. Soft toys for young children should be well made, with small parts tightly secured.

☐ The Consumer Product Safety Commission does not recommend toys with sharp points or edges, or electric toys with heating elements, for children under age eight.

☐ Toys that shoot objects can injure eyes. Avoid them.

☐ Avoid toys with long strings or cords, which pose a strangulation hazard.

☐ Keep all toys with small parts away from children under age three, as well as from any older children who still put toys in their mouths.

☐ Small balls and toys with small ball-like parts are a choking hazard and should not be given to young children.

☐ Remember: Nothing replaces supervision.

FOR MORE INFORMATION

☐ The U.S. Consumer Product Safety Commission has many free booklets. To receive a complete index, write to the Office of Information and Public Affairs, U.S. Consumer Products Safety Commission, Washington, D.C. 20207, or call (800) 638-CPSC from anywhere in the continental U.S.

☐ The following pamphlets are available free from CPSC: "Which Toy for Which Child: A Consumer's Guide for Selecting Suitable Toys." Ask for the birth to five-year-olds edition. "F.S. 47 Toys," "F.S. 61 Electric Toys," "F.S. 74 Toy Chests," "Toy Safety Coloring Book" (English and Spanish). Write: Office of Information and Public Affairs, U.S. Consumer Products Safety Commission, Washington, D.C. 20207.

Arts/Crafts/Making Things

☐ Keep all art supplies (paints, markers, etc.) in one box, out of reach. Have another box for collage materials.

☐ If you've got an impetuous artist on your hands, restrict

the crayons and paint to the high chair till he can control himself.

☐ If your toddler cannot resist writing on the walls, the following will satisfy the urge and keep your walls clean: Buy two yards of white, pressure-sensitive wall covering and place it at a convenient height on a wall. Frame the edges with colored tape. The drawings your child makes on it with wax crayons can be wiped away with a paper towel.

☐ If you're out of fingerpaint paper, use the shiny side of freezer wrap.

☐ For sewing fun, punch holes in clean foam trays from meat packages. Use an old shoelace for thread, or wrap one end of yarn with masking tape to make a "needle."

☐ Newspaper is the only paper you need for a beginning painter.

☐ Unwaxed white shelf paper is great for drawing and painting, and it's inexpensive.

☐ Give your child only one color to paint with at first. If you give more than one, she'll probably just mix them together and paint with the mixture.

☐ Recycle egg cartons as paint holders.

☐ Save your yogurt cups and tops. They are perfect containers for paint, because the tops keep paint from drying out, and they fit into the easel tray.

☐ Plastic mustard and ketchup bottles are handy containers for paint and glue.

☐ Go beyond the paintbrush. Let your child paint with sponges, cotton swabs, cotton balls, string or pipe cleaners.

☐ On those days when you just can't face a painting project, pull out the paint-with-water books. All you need is a brush and water. These are great for traveling.

☐ Try finger-painting in the bathtub for easy cleanup.

☐ Mix a little dishwashing liquid into finger paints; it will make cleanup much easier.

☐ Use baby oil or baby lotion to clean paint or colored marker off your child's skin.

☐ Mix food coloring with hand cream for body paint that comes off easily in the bath.

☐ Don't forget colored chalk for driveways, sidewalks or front steps. A bucket of water or the rain cleans it up easily.

☐ If your toddler can't resist tasting, have her finger-paint with chocolate pudding or whipped cream (add food coloring if you like). One mother squirts it on the refrigerator door for her child.

☐ On every sheet of stamps there's a blank row of stamps. Be sure to get your artist in residence to decorate these and stick them on *his* letters.

☐ Toddlers prefer washable markers to crayons.

☐ When gluing, it's neater if *you* drop the glue on the paper and let your child mash whatever he wants on top of it.

☐ Let your child use a glue stick for collages of paper or very light materials.

☐ Preinked stamp pads usually contain permanent ink. To make your own stamp pad, use an old sink sponge moistened with any color paint. This works best if the paint is fairly thick and the sponge is not completely soaked.

☐ Use alphabet blocks that have a raised design for stamping.

☐ Make stamps from art gum erasers. Draw the design on one side. Then cut away the material outside the design with a single-edge razor blade. Use short strokes.

☐ Many household objects can be used for stamps and make wonderful designs: corks, pinecones, sponges cut into shapes, bottle tops, marker caps, toy pieces.

☐ Necklaces can be made by stringing buttons, various shapes of pasta or cut-up straws. Put tape or glue on the end of the string to make it stiff enough to poke through.

☐ Use the back of your child's pictures as stationery when writing to Grandma.

☐ The cardboard rolls from paper towels makes good mailers for your child's artwork.

☐ Use straight pins to attach your child's pictures to the walls of his room if the walls are made of plasterboard. The holes are practically invisible, so there's a lot less damage than with tape or thumbtacks. Just hang the pictures high enough so that children can't pull the pins out.

☐ To display your child's artwork, stretch string along the walls like a clothesline, anchor it and hang paintings on it with tape, paper clips or clothespins.

☐ Date all your child's artwork as it's done.

☐ The following are good places to get free or low-cost art supplies:

- Home decorating stores: fabric and wallpaper samples
- Cabinetmakers, building supply stores, furniture builders, college or high school theater departments: scrap wood
- Printing shops: paper of all sorts
- Upholstery shops: fabric samples
- Newspaper offices: leftover ends of plain newsprint

TWO PLAY DOUGH RECIPES

☐ Homemade play dough is often easier to clean up than the commercial kind, and it smells better. Here is one of the best of many versions:

1 cup flour
½ cup salt
2 tablespoons oil
2 teaspoons cream of tartar
1 cup water
a few drops of food coloring (if desired)

Mix all ingredients in a pot, then cook over medium heat. Stir till thick (about 4 minutes). Knead while warm. Store in a sealed plastic bag or other airtight container.

☐ This recipe doesn't have the wonderful texture and firmness of the cooked play dough just given, but it's easy, and you're bound to have all the ingredients on hand.

3 cups flour
1 cup salt

1 cup warm water
2 tbs. vegetable oil
a few drops of food coloring (if desired)

Mix all ingredients and knead. If it's too sticky, add more flour. Store in an airtight container.

☐ To preserve your child's play-dough sculptures, bake them in a 300-degree oven for a half hour to an hour or more (depending on the thickness of the dough) until hard. Hollow out thick pieces as best you can before baking. They can be painted after baking. Coat them with shellac or a clear acrylic fixative so that they will not absorb moisture.

☐ Let your child use the following with play dough:

- garlic press
- potato ricer
- cookie cutters
- dull table knife
- rolling pin
- anything that will stamp interesting patterns: bottle caps, sieves, potato mashers

Things to Do on a Rainy Day

☐ Bowl. Make a bowling set, using plastic cups or empty plastic bottles and a large ball. A hallway is a good place to set up your bowling alley.

☐ It's grand fun to draw on a picture window with soap, and your child will gladly wash it when he's through.

- [ ] Boxes, pans or pails make good targets for bean bags or foam balls.

- [ ] Indoor playhouses can be made by throwing a sheet over a table.

- [ ] Have an Easter egg hunt with tennis balls, nuts or the like.

- [ ] Tape-record your child's voice and/or you telling a story.

- [ ] With a paper punch, make all kinds of crazy designs. Collect the punched circles for collages.

- [ ] Sort your photos and let your child help you put them in an album.

- [ ] Clean a closet. Your child will almost always find something intriguing to play with.

- [ ] Create a personalized neighborhood for your child's toy cars. Draw it on posterboard and cover it with clear adhesive vinyl. Traffic signs can be bought or made.

- [ ] Put a large amount of salt in a cake pan. Your child can draw pictures and letters in it. Just shake the pan to erase.

- [ ] Save your child's artwork in a box and pull it out for a rainy day art show.

- [ ] Have an indoor picnic. Pack up everything in a picnic basket and spread out a blanket in the living room.

- [ ] Make your own puzzles. Glue a picture on heavy cardboard. Cover it with clear, pressure-sensitive vinyl and cut. A three-year-old will be happy to make a puzzle for you while you make one for her.

☐ Blow up balloons for a game of baseball or soccer.

Learning Games

As one mother pointed out, almost everything you do is a learning game. For instance, you probably count the stairs as you go up and down and count raisins as you give them out. Do you also count how many have been eaten and how many are left?

☐ Letters can be associated with people, for example, *D* is David's letter, *M* is Mommy's letter.

☐ Magnetized letters and numbers on the refrigerator can spell out a word a day (or week), can be grouped by color, can be turned upside down or sideways to make new letters and the like.

☐ Always point out and read frequently seen signs, such as STOP, NO EXIT, ONE WAY.

☐ An inexpensive calculator can help with numbers and counting.

☐ Paint two sets of numbers on your basement steps, one to look at as you go down, the other as you go up.

☐ Tape favorite pictures at your child's eye level and point out new things each time you look at them.

☐ Write down the stories your child dictates. Print all the words so your child will begin to recognize them.

☐ Try a Directions game. Give one short direction ("Touch your nose"). Upon completion, add another ("Touch your nose, jump three times"), then another.

☐ A good game to play when you're waiting for a meal: "I see something on this table that's yellow and begins with the letter *M*. Can you guess what it is?" Use color clues, shape clues, texture clues, etc.

General Observations

☐ When you have a toddler, you no longer have to throw away junk mail! Tell him it's for him; he will love to open it all. Use paper not printed on the back for drawing and coloring, cut out colorful pictures from circulars, make paper airplanes.

☐ Create a winter sandbox from a plastic swimming pool or an old baby bath. Put it on a plastic tablecloth or sheet for quick cleanup.

☐ Children love to jump on beds and furniture. Instead of always saying no, set up an old mattress on the floor, cover it with a pretty sheet and call it their jumping mattress.

☐ Keep the Halloween costumes available all year round for dress-up. Add some of Mom and Dad's old clothes and shoes.

☐ If you let your child use your makeup, watch for allergic reactions. Even face cream can cause a reaction.

☐ Record as much as you can of your child's early talking. Not only will you preserve wonderful memories, but the recordings are sure to amuse your child now and later in life.

☐ A personal photo album can be a child's greatest treasure. Get duplicates of the best pictures of your child,

relatives, pets, friends. Buy an album that has plastic pages for the pictures so they'll stay clean. Or mount pictures on cardboard, cover with clear, pressure-sensitive vinyl and make your own book.

☐ Kids *love* to play with coins. They can sort them, stack them, learn numbers with them. Be sure children keep them out of their mouths, though.

☐ Most scissors made for children are worthless and frustrating for them to use. Get small but good adult scissors instead and *supervise* their use.

☐ Your child can use the baby scissors with the rounded tips you bought to cut her nails.

☐ Plastic safety scissors for children made with a thin metal strip instead of a metal blade do cut well.

☐ If your child is left-handed, be sure to buy special scissors made for lefties. They make a big difference.

☐ Use yarn or string to tie your child's scissors to her art table. She'll never lose them and never be tempted to run with them in her hand.

☐ Sharpen scissors by cutting sandpaper with them.

13

Birthdays and Holidays

Birthdays

The most often repeated birthday advice: for headache-free parties, match the number of guests to your child's years: two guests for a two-year-old, three guests for a three-year-old. Of course, that advice should be tempered with your perception of your own stamina, the child's personality and her heartfelt desires. If she wants 10 nursery-school friends at her party, you may have no choice!

THE SECOND BIRTHDAY

☐ For a two, an adult- or family-only party is plenty. Maybe have one or two children with parents over if you must, but don't be elaborate.

☐ The best present you could give your child is a party at which he's the only guest and he gets to play with his Mom and Dad exclusively.

☐ One opinion: *"Birthday parties for two-year-olds are an exercise in frustration. Every one I have witnessed has*

195

ended with the birthday child in tears. The party is really for you."

The foregoing represents general feelings about birthday parties for twos. Don't feel guilty about keeping things simple; just save your energy for:

THE THIRD AND FOURTH BIRTHDAYS

- [ ] Think of your child's needs first; after all, it is her day. If she's best in the morning, have the party then. If some relatives have to miss it, so be it. Be firm!

- [ ] Don't prepare your child for a party more than a few days in advance. Otherwise you'll be plagued with endless questions and might even end up with a child who is sick from excitement on the day of the party.

- [ ] Do write "play clothes" on your birthday invitations if you intend to have the children play outside (or if you want to indicate that your party is informal).

- [ ] A great birthday table idea: place a large sheet of plywood on six 1-gallon paint cans. Cover it with a pretty sheet. The children sit on the floor and love it!

- [ ] Instead of seating children at a table, just lay a tablecloth or two on the floor for a "picnic." Advantages: No one gets hurt falling off chairs (it happens), and you can seat any number of children. Disadvantage: The children may tend to hop up more and run around. It depends on your group.

- [ ] As the guests arrive, let your child unwrap each gift in the presence of the giver and give her thank-yous. As soon as you can (maybe while the children are being seated at the table), put the gifts away so they are not appropriated and/or broken by the guests. Have plenty of other toys available for play.

☐ To keep everybody busy until the last guest arrives, give out pages of coloring books and paper cups with crayons. Or spread out a long piece of white paper on the floor, distribute crayons and have party guests create a mural.

☐ Have an older sibling or a familiar baby-sitter help with your toddler's birthday party. Preteen girls are especially good at getting down on the floor and really playing with toddlers. This frees you for other things. The children will be thrilled if the helper wears clown makeup or dresses as a cartoon character.

☐ Parents will enjoy the party much more if they arrange to have someone (a relative, a neighbor) take the pictures.

☐ Sometimes the birthday child is devastated when all his friends leave after a much-anticipated birthday party. You might arrange to have one good friend stay a bit after the others go to cushion the blow.

☐ If you want the party to end exactly on time (and who doesn't), drive the guests home.

Special Party Ideas

☐ Take everybody fishing! Their favor is their own little fishing pole made from a dowel or branch.

☐ Have a clown party. All the children come in hobo clothes. Put clown makeup on their faces as they arrive. Put out some mirrors so they can add their own decorations. Encourage tattoos, also!

☐ Set up a carnival in your backyard. (Older siblings are a big help with this.) Make sure the games are easy, so all children can win.

☐ Reverse the seasons and/or holidays. Have a Christmas-type party in July. Or dress up like Halloween in May. (Four-year-olds can really get a kick out of the silliness of this; threes may be a bit young.)

☐ Have guests come as what they want to be when they grow up.

☐ Have the party at a family-oriented restaurant. Prices are usually reasonable, and the kids really love this kind of party.

☐ Borrow story filmstrips from the library, and the projector as well. Many filmstrips will tie in with a "theme" or holiday party. Or borrow a video cartoon.

Preparty Activities

You may wish to involve your child in:

- Making/selecting the birthday invitations and mailing them.
- Making/selecting party favors and wrapping them.
- Making/selecting the party decorations.
- Cleaning the house.
- Setting the table.
- Baking/decorating the cake.

Note: Only if you have great patience should you involve a pretwo in these activities.

Preparty Activities

☐ Be sure you give the same favors—the *same* plastic dinosaur, not different ones. Otherwise some child is sure to want what another has.

☐ Consider wrapping a number of little favors for each guest. Then, while the birthday child opens her gifts, the guests will have things to unwrap, too.

☐ For a warm-weather outdoor party, use sand buckets as favors. Write the child's name on them and they're place cards. Fill them with goodies and they'll anchor the paper plates.

☐ An instant photograph of each child at a birthday party is a wonderful favor. If you can get the guests to put on makeup or costumes, they're even more fun. Be sure to let each child watch his picture develop.

☐ Help your child make individualized place mats on heavy paper for each guest. Cover with clear adhesive vinyl and give them to guests as souvenirs.

☐ One mother, who gave whistles as favors, confided to parents as they departed, *"They break easily if you 'accidentally' step on them."*

☐ Give favors in a sealed "loot bag" just as the children are leaving. Ask them not to open it until they're in the car. That way nothing gets lost, and the child is motivated to leave the party quickly!

Food

A general rule: the simpler the better, and not much. Most children will be too excited to eat.

☐ Serve individual pizzas made on English muffins.

☐ Cut sandwiches into animal shapes with cookie cutters.

☐ Health-food stores have lots of alternatives to candy: honeyed banana chips, dried fruit, nuts, and so on.

☐ If you have a cake, make sure there is a flower on *each* piece to eliminate arguments over who gets the flower. Twos and threes must have exactly the same of everything.

☐ Use candy with a hole in the middle for birthday candle holders, or stick candles in soft, gummy candy.

☐ Instead of cake, try:

- *Clown cones:* Dip a sugar cone in melted chocolate to coat rim. Cool. Put scoop of ice cream on plate. Top with cone for hat. Squirt whipped cream for hair. Use raisins or cherries for eyes, nose and mouth.
- *Cupcakes:* They're easier to eat, and there will be no argument over size. Try baking them in flat-bottom ice cream cones as a special treat. Or leave the frosting off and let the kids frost them themselves. Put out containers of toppings (sprinkles, raisins, etc.), too.
- *Ice-cream cake:* This two-in-one is very popular with children. It saves messy scooping and eliminates some waste. Most two- and three-year-olds can't eat a full serving of cake *and* a scoop of ice cream.

- *Ice-cream sundaes:* Put small scoops (use a melon-ball maker) of different flavors of ice cream into bowls and leave the toppings on the table (nuts, syrups, sprinkles) for children to dig into themselves.
- Light one *big* candle for the child to blow out. You can buy a candle in the shape of a number of his age.

☐ Consider saving the birthday cake for the birthday dinner with just the family.

Party Activities for Third and Fourth Birthdays

From one parent: *"The best advice I ever got was to overplan. Have enough activities to fill all the time and then some. You probably won't finish, but it avoids having three- and four-year-olds tearing around your home without any purpose except trouble. They are wonderful when busy."*

If the children make anything at your party, be sure to write their name on it as they're doing it, so there will be no last-minute mix-ups before leaving.

The approximate time each activity will take is given in parentheses.

☐ Have children decorate their own party hats. Cut paper to size with about two inches to spare (use your own child as a model), and give one flat piece to each child. The guests should have their own piles of cutout pictures (from toy catalogs, comic books), stickers, stars, crayons and the like. Mom or Dad is the glue keeper and drops glue upon request. Crepe-paper ruffles or streamers can be taped on. When the creation is complete, tape or staple the hat together. (20 minutes)

☐ Make masks. Beforehand, glue a stick to a white paper plate and supply the glue and precut eyes, mouths, ears and decorations to each child. (15 minutes)

☐ Guests will enjoy decorating a container to hold all their loot. Dig into your junk box and supply them with decorative material: paper, markers, glue-on stuff, scissors. Use shoe boxes, Chinese take-out containers, mushroom baskets—all of which will be more substantial than flimsy bags. (15 minutes)

☐ Let guests "fish" for their favors. Create some kind of dry "pool" out of blocks or whatever. Wrap each favor so that a big loop of ribbon sticks up. Make a fishing pole with a *large* hook on the end. Each child takes turns fishing (it takes longer that way) while the others watch. (15 minutes)

☐ Everyone loves a peanut hunt. Just hide peanuts in one room and let the kids loose. Have lots of extras on hand in case one child can't find any. (10 minutes)

☐ Give a puppet show. For a stage, stretch paper or fabric across a door frame. Children love to be talked to by puppets. And be sure to have a puppet give out the favors. (20 minutes or as long as you can last)

☐ Have children make their own gingerbread men—one to eat at the party and one to take home. Supply precut forms and all decorations: raisins, candied orange slices, nuts, sprinkles. Bake during lunch. (10 minutes)

☐ Animal charades are good fun. Each child pretends to be an animal and the others guess what it is. You can keep going as long as it amuses the guests.

☐ Plan to end the birthday party by reading a story or two to the group. This will help keep things from going out of control.

☐ The library will have records and tapes with activity songs you can play at the end of the party.

☐ Don't forget old favorites from your childhood that you can teach the children, such as "London Bridge" or "Hokey Pokey."

☐ Hire a magician for a magic show to end the party.

Keep in Mind

☐ Children can get frightened with too much attention suddenly focused on them. *"On his third birthday, my son burst into tears when we all started singing 'Happy Birthday' and would not let us continue."*

☐ Any game that requires two- and three-year-old children to be blindfolded is usually a flop. Many of them simply will not want their eyes covered.

☐ Don't be surprised if there's not much interest in organized games. Activities (see foregoing) seem to appeal more than such games as Pin the Tail on the Donkey.

☐ Avoid any games in which there's a winner. It's hard for anyone of this age to lose. Who needs tears?

☐ Tears also result when balloons pop. Have *plenty* around so each child can leave with one. And have some extras for siblings of guests who come with parents at the end of the party.

☐ If children create something at your party to take home, have them make it before they eat. Collect these treasures before sitting down at the table, and whisk them away to be returned as the children leave. Otherwise damage, loss and tears might result.

Going to Birthday Parties

☐ Let your child give as birthday gifts the toys he likes at home. Since he already has a duplicate, it won't be hard to give the gift away.

☐ Do your hostess a favor and don't bring presents that are noisy or have lots of small pieces.

☐ As long as you're out shopping for one birthday gift, buy several at the same time. Once your child goes to nursery school, she'll be invited to lots of parties, and it's nice to have presents in reserve.

General Observations

☐ To preserve treasured holiday and birthday cards, arrange them on a piece of colored construction paper and cover both sides with clear, pressure-sensitive vinyl to make very special placemats.

☐ At holiday time, your child will probably be enchanted with only one or two toys. Put the others away in their boxes and bring them out later when they will brighten a rainy day.

☐ Make a reusable birthday tablecloth. Buy a solid color tablecloth and draw or stencil a big HAPPY BIRTHDAY on it with permanent marker or fabric paint. (The color may go through the tablecloth, so always write with something underneath.) Use the tablecloth at each family birthday dinner, and let parents and children write or draw something with permanent marker at each celebration. It will bring back wonderful memories each time you use it.

☐ Birthdays will be less stressful if parents, siblings, grandparents and friends remember that toddlers can get very excited. Don't talk too much about the party in advance. Keep the planning and preparation fairly low key so that your child will be able to sleep and nap on schedule and really enjoy the celebration.

Special Gifts

For a nifty gift, how about a special "adoption"? Write to these organizations for free information:

☐ For "So You'd Like to Adopt a Wild Horse or Burro," write: Consumer Information Center-V, P.O. Box 100, Pueblo, CO 81002.

☐ The Izaak Walton League of America, 1401 Wilson BL, Level B, Arlington, VA 22209, will give you information on how to adopt a stream if you send them a self-addressed, stamped envelope.

☐ Adopt a zoo animal. Contact the Public Relations department of your local zoo to see if there is an animal adoption program.

☐ Want a whale? Write: Adopt a Right Whale Program, New England Aquarium, Central Wharf, Boston, MA 02110-3399.

Holidays

☐ To make the waiting for a special holiday more pleasant:
- If it's at all possible, don't even mention that a holiday is coming up until about a week or so before it occurs. Toddlers have little sense of time and can wear themselves (and you) into a frazzle of anticipation.
- You and your child can design a special calendar with large dates that can be scribbled out by the child as the big day approaches.
- Glue 10 (or more) wooden match boxes together, decorate, fill each with a surprise and open one a day.
- Four days before the holiday each family member gets to do one wacky thing a day (with parental approval, of course), perhaps have cereal for dinner or wearing pjs all day. If you feel your children might get too imaginative with this, make a list of wacky things to choose from.

☐ Parents are so used to holidays and their traditions, they often forget to tell two- and three-year-olds exactly what to expect. Children can be disappointed unless they have a very clear idea of what will happen or rules you expect to be followed. (For example, birthday gifts will be opened *after* breakfast, or Halloween candy cannot be eaten all at once.) It's a good idea to repeat the sequence of events fairly often.

☐ It's nice to have holiday treasures that are brought out year after year to decorate the dining-room table, front door or other parts of your home. Ceramic Halloween pumpkins are an example, or your homemade Easter basket. Children truly enjoy continuity and tradition. You will be surprised how much your three-year-old remembers from her second year.

☐ Make your own Family Awards Night holiday. The categories are announced ("For the child who makes the best scrambled eggs and knows the whole alphabet"), and everyone guesses who the winner will be. This encourages good habits, rewards special efforts and generally makes everyone feel just great. Needless to say, all children get awards. (The parent whose idea this is does it on Valentine's Day.)

☐ Save the holiday cards for next year. Have children cut out the pictures and paste them on colored paper to make their own cards and wrapping paper.

☐ Those crayon masterpieces can be turned into great holiday gift wrap for children's presents to others. (That gets them off your refrigerator.)

☐ A box filled with oddments such as Styrofoam pellets, sequins, macaroni, buttons and the like is fun to get out at gift-wrapping time so your child can decorate the presents he's going to give in a unique way.

☐ Help your child make gifts for the family. Although she may not be truly enthusiastic about the idea and you may have to do most of the work, you will be rewarded by her joy and pride as Grandma praises her beautiful paperweight. Here are some ideas:

   • Play dough (see recipes for the homemade kind on

- pages 188–189) can be shaped into ashtrays, candy dishes, paperweights, coin holders and so on.
- Flatten a lump of play dough. Have your child make a handprint in it. Carve the child's name and date into the dough. One easy way to write letters in play dough is to make them out of tiny holes pricked into the dough with a nail.
- Cut a gingerbread man out of play dough. Cut a circle into the dough where the face should be, and glue on a picture of your child's face so it will show through the hole. Note: To preserve these treasures, homemade play dough should be baked at 300°F for about an hour or until hard. Paint can then be applied if desired. Shellac or spray with an acrylic fixative to prevent moisture absorption and crumbling.
- Glue ice-pop sticks together to make a frame for a photograph of your child. Have the child decorate the frame with paint, sparkles, shells and the like.
- Frame "portraits" of relatives drawn by your child and attach some thoughts about them (which have been dictated to you) on the back.
- A juice can turns into an attractive pencil holder when nicely adorned.
- Personally decorated cookies (or any food you two enjoy making) are always a treat.

☐ It's nice if gift-giving holidays include a family participation game as one of the gifts, so that after all the excitement dies down, there's something you can all do together.

☐ Even toddlers can be affected by holiday stress. Don't get so caught up in preparations that you spend less time with your child. If anything, you need more time alone with each other.

☐ Be sure to plan some treats for the children *after* the holiday. This helps prevent the postholiday blues.

Holiday Safety Tips

☐ Don't forget to stick reflective strips on your child's Halloween costume for after dark safety.

☐ Many holiday plants are poisonous. These include holly and mistletoe berries, boxwood leaves, ivy leaves and the entire Jerusalem cherry plant. The poinsettia can cause irritation to the skin, mouth and stomach. Call your Poison Control Center for further information if *any* plant is eaten.

☐ Avoid decorations that look like candy or food.

☐ Strings of popcorn and cranberries are a choking hazard to toddlers.

☐ Decorations within reach must be nonbreakable.

☐ Attach the Christmas tree to the walls with wire to prevent a child from pulling it down.

☐ Put your Christmas tree in the playpen.

☐ Tree decorations that look like toys are *not* made for children to play with, but children find them irresistible. They can break, splinter, be swallowed and chewed on. Put them way up and out of reach or avoid them altogether.

☐ Keep those fire salts (that produce colored flames) out of children's reach.

- [ ] Select tinsel or artificial icicles of plastic or nonleaded metals, and hang them out of reach.

- [ ] Never let children play with sparklers or firecrackers.

- [ ] Clean up gift wrap quickly. Loose ribbons and wrap could cause children to trip or choke.

- [ ] Be extra mindful of your child when visiting friends or family who have older children or no children at home. They may have dangerous things where your toddler can get them.

- [ ] For more safety tips, see Chapter 4, "Safety and Health."

FOR MORE INFORMATION

- [ ] For the free booklet "Halloween Fire Safety," write: Office of Information and Public Affairs, U.S. Consumer Products Safety Commission, Washington, D.C. 20207, or call (800) 638-CPSC from anywhere in the continental U.S. Ask for booklet F.S. 100. While you're at it, ask for their booklet "Merry Christmas with Safety" for holiday safety.

- [ ] Call (800) 621-7619 Ext. 1300 to order "Don't Be Afraid on Halloween," #59977-0000, a guide for parents to teach children safe trick-or-treating, or write to the National Safety Council, 444 N. Michigan Ave., Chicago, IL 60611.

- [ ] The National Child Safety Council in Jackson, Mississippi, publishes brochures that are available through your local police department or sheriff's office. Call the police department in your area to find out what they have or if they can obtain information on a particular subject of interest to you.

14

Nursery School

Choosing a School

☐ Points to consider when looking for a nursery school or play care:

- Your child is an individual who may thrive in a certain atmosphere but wither in another. Just because your neighbors send their child to a certain school does *not* mean it will be right for your child.
- Visit several schools and stay long enough to observe different activities. Remember that the teachers' first responsibility is to the children, so if they don't have time to answer your questions while you're visiting, ask when it would be convenient for you to call them.
- Ask the teachers about their philosophy and objectives. Do they stress social development? (Your child may be very comfortable with peers already and may need more stimulation.) What are their methods of discipline—for example, how would they handle disruptive behavior? (Your child may be having frequent temper tantrums.) Think of as many specific questions as you can.

213

- How many children are there per teacher? (Ten children would seem to be the maximum any adult could handle.)
- What are the teachers' backgrounds? Remember that extensive teaching experience with another age group does not necessarily mean that they are good with two- and three-year-olds.
- Are the children separated by age groups or do they all share the same classroom? If the latter is the case, how does the school cope with physically active threes and quiet, curious fours, for instance?
- Are school trips planned? How are the children transported? Are seat restraints required on trips?
- Ask how the parents are kept informed of their child's progress. Do teachers keep daily notes on each child? What are their record-keeping methods?
- Check for emergency exits and ask if the school holds regularly scheduled fire drills.
- The atmosphere created by the teachers is far more important than the amount of toys or equipment they have.

☐ In some places, particularly urban areas, you have to register for nursery schools a *year* in advance. Keep this in mind.

Before School Begins

☐ Take your child past the building often, and always mention that he'll be going to school there next fall.

☐ If possible, take your child to the school's playground and let her get familiar with at least one aspect of her new school.

☐ While school is still in session, visit *with* your child for an hour or so. Quite often this will create happy memories you can discuss during the summer.

☐ Tell your child exactly what routine to expect, and tell him what *you'll* be doing while he's in school.

First Days

☐ Many children are afraid that Mommy will not come back to pick them up but cannot articulate this fear. Be sure you frequently reassure the child that you are coming back. You might point to a clock and show the child where the hands will be when you come for him.

☐ Keep stressing that you'll pick him up for *lunch* rather than using a time like twelve o'clock, because most children won't have any idea when that is.

☐ Before you drop her off at school, talk about what you're going to do together *after* school.

☐ Sometimes the first week goes smoothly; it's the second week when crying and fussing start. Be prepared to ride this out. It does stop if you're firm and secure in your decision and the school handles it well.

☐ If you want to make sure the crying stops (even though the teachers assure you it does), stand outside the door *(out of sight)* for a while.

General Observations

☐ If you have a child who is just (or not quite) three in September, consider carefully before you put him in nursery school. One mother writes: *"My friends who put*

their 'just threes' in nursery school were sorry. They weren't ready for it."

☐ Calling a play group school makes it much more attractive to little ones.

☐ Don't be surprised if your child imitates the worst-behaved child in the group. That child may be attracting a lot of attention from the adults in the room as well as from the other children.

☐ Ask how your school handles emergencies so that you can act most efficiently if a crisis arises.

☐ Make sure your school will not let the child go home with anyone but you unless you've approved it in person or by written note.

☐ *"I've become much more aware of the danger of children being sexually abused. One of the tips the police and social workers give is that we must be careful not to ignore our children. We must learn to pay close attention to what they say and how they are behaving. If we do, our children will know that they can come to us with a problem. I ignored my three-year-old crying and not wanting to go to school. After two months, I found out he was being bullied by a six-year-old and the playground teachers had not noticed it."*

15

First Aid

Emergencies and Minor Accidents

These first-aid procedures are not intended as a substitute for a doctor's care, but they will help you cope with a crisis before you can reach a doctor or other medical assistance. Please read these instructions now and familiarize yourself with them.

Some especially important procedures have been marked this way: ■; they call for immediate action on your part. As a responsible parent you should study what to do *now*, before an accident. You do not want to have to read about choking as your child is turning blue.

The best advice is: *Don't panic, stay calm*. This will not only help you cope quickly and sensibly but will also reassure and calm your child.

ABRASIONS

☐ First soak in warm, soapy water. Put your child in the bath, if necessary. Gently clean the scraped skin. Be sure to remove any loose particles of dirt.

☐ Apply antiseptic, then an antibiotic ointment or cream.

☐ Cover the scrape with a sterile dressing.

☐ If the dirt is too deep for you to remove painlessly, ask your doctor to do it using a local anesthetic.

BEE OR OTHER INSECT STINGS

■ If the child begins to have any difficulty breathing, she must have medical care immediately. Rush to the nearest doctor or hospital emergency room. Call the police and get them to drive you there if necessary. They may be able to administer some emergency measures, as well. (Some children have an allergic reaction to stings that causes their throats to swell. They must be treated quickly before they suffocate.)

■ If any other allergic reactions appear (for example, hives or vomiting), call your doctor right away.

☐ Relieve the itch or sting with ice cubes, calomine lotion, a paste of bicarbonate of soda or meat tenderizer (mix the powder with a few drops of water), vinegar or nonprescription hydrocortisone ointment. If it's a bee sting, remove the stinger by scraping it out with a tweezer cleaned with alcohol or soap and water.

BITES

Animal

☐ Control bleeding if necessary. (See "Cuts," pages 225–226.)

☐ Wash thoroughly with soap and water, apply antiseptic and cover with sterile bandage.

☐ Call your pediatrician.

☐ The animal must be tested for rabies, so either keep track of it or call the police to help capture it.

Human

☐ Same treatment as for animal bites if the skin is broken. Don't forget to call the doctor.

Tick

☐ Tiny deer ticks can spread Lyme disease. If you see a tick on your child, do the following:

- Remove the tick gently with tweezers; do not kill it before removal. Save the tick for possible analysis.
- Clean the bite with antiseptic.
- Watch for the following symptoms: a red area or rash near the bite, fever, headache, joint pains, fatigue, stiff neck. If you suspect Lyme disease, take your child to your doctor immediately.

BREATHING: ARTIFICIAL RESPIRATION

■ Get someone to summon medical help. (Call the police, then your doctor.)

■ Proceed *only* if child is *not* beathing.

■ Clear the child's mouth of debris with your finger. Be careful not to push any possible obstruction into her throat.

■ With the child on his back, place your hand under his neck and gently tip his head back to open the air passage. Chin must be *up*.

■ With your ear to the child's mouth, listen for breathing to begin. If it does not:

■ Cover the child's mouth and nose with your mouth and puff *some* air into the child's mouth. His lungs are much smaller than yours, so use only a partial breath.

■ Put your ear to the child's mouth and listen for air coming out.

- *If air comes out:*

    Continue breathing gently into his lungs at a rate of about one new breath every three to five seconds.

    Take your mouth away between breaths to allow air to be expelled.

    Keep this up until the child can breathe by himself.

- *If no air comes out:*

    Try another breath. Watch the chest to see if it rises. If no air is getting into the lungs, there may be a throat obstruction.

    Remove obstruction. (See "Choking," pages 223–224.)

    Return the child onto his back. Tilt his head again to point the chin up.

    Begin artificial respiration again. (See column at left.)

BUMPS AND BRUISES

☐ Relieve the pain with an ice cube (wrapped in a cloth or a plastic bag) and a kiss.

BURNS

Serious burns (third degree—resulting in white or charred skin—or extensive second-degree burns):

If clothes catch fire, roll the child in something to smother the flames (a coat, a blanket, a rug, a tablecloth).

Never let a child run with burning clothes.

Cover burned skin with a clean cloth or a sheet.

☐ Get medical help immediately. (Rush to the nearest physician or emergency room; call the police if you need transportation.)

☐ Treat for shock. (See "Shock," page 229.)

Minor burns (first and second degree—resulting in red skin and/or blisters):

Run cold water over burned skin immediately (or apply wet cold compresses). Continue until pain subsides. And for anything but very minor burns, seek medical attention right away.

☐ Cover burned skin with a sterile bandage.

☐ Do not apply any ointment (first aid creams, sprays, butter, grease, etc.) to burns.

☐ Do not pop blisters.

CHOKING

Never interfere with a child's own attempts to cough or clear her own throat.

Turn the child upside down to help shake the object out. Give her a sharp slap or two on the back.

If the child can breathe but cannot expel the object he's swallowed, get medical help immediately.

■ If you can see the object, pull it out. Be careful not to push it farther down the throat.

To remove obstruction if the child cannot breathe:

■ Place the child head-down over your knees. Give three or four sharp blows between the shoulder blades with the heel of your hand.

■ If the obstruction is not ejected, get behind the child and wrap your arms around his middle. Make a fist with one hand and cover it with the other. Place your fist between the ribs and the navel and thrust upward sharply four times. Repeat procedure if necessary.

☐ Administer artificial respiration if necessary. (See "Breathing: Artificial Respiration," pages 221–222.)

CONVULSIONS

■ If the child is hot, see "Febrile Convulsions," page 226.

☐ Scary as they are to see, most convulsions stop by themselves. Observe the child's movements carefully and call the doctor. Only if a convulsion lasts more than five minutes or if the child goes from one into another do you need emergency help.

CROUP

Croup without fever:

■ Take the child into the bathroom and run hot water in the shower to make steam. Or if it's cool outside (50° F [10° C] or less) bundle him up and take him outside. Both methods should stop spasms.

■ If breathing does *not* improve after a few minutes, call police for emergency aid or rush to the nearest emergency room.

☐ After regular breathing is restored, humidify air in the child's room with vaporizer or humidifier. He should breathe moist air for several nights after croup.

Croup with fever:

■ Call the pediatrician for instructions. See foregoing methods for making breathing easier for the child. If you are not able to reach a doctor quickly and have a breathing emergency, call police or rush to the nearest emergency room.

CUTS

Wounds bleeding severely:

■ Any large flow of blood must be stopped immediately.

■ Cover the wound with a sterile or clean cloth (or just your hand if nothing else is available) and press the wound with your hand to control bleeding.

■ Still pressing, raise the injured part of the body higher than the heart if possible.

■ When bleeding is under control, bandage the wound firmly.

☐ Seek medical care immediately.

Minor cuts and scratches:

☐ Control bleeding. (See foregoing instructions.)

☐ If the cut is deep enough to see the tissues under the skin, if the edges are ragged or if the cut is on the face, call your doctor for further advice.

☐ Wash carefully with soap and water to remove all dirt. Apply antiseptic and antibiotic ointment.

☐ If the cut is small, *clean* and you want to hold the edges together, use a butterfly bandage. Otherwise use a regular bandage to keep dirt out.

DROWNING

■ Have someone else get medical help immediately.

■ Drain water from the lungs by tilting body head-down for about 8 to 10 seconds.

■ Administer artificial respiration. (See "Breathing: Artificial Respiration," pages 221–222.)

FALLS

See "Head Injuries," page 227.

FEBRILE CONVULSIONS (convulsions caused by high fever)

■ Cool the child off quickly. Douse him under cool running water, clothes and all.

■ Stay with the child. Have someone else call a doctor immediately; if this is not possible, wrap the child in a wet towel and make the call yourself.

■ If convulsions continue after a minute or two, call police or rush to the emergency room. Do not wait to hear from the doctor.

FEVER

☐ If the fever is over 101° F (38.5° C), call your doctor.

■ If you can't reach the doctor and the fever has reached 103° F (39° C) or more, it should be brought down. Use this method: Bathe the child in lukewarm water in a tub or give a sponge bath for 20 minutes or so. Do not let the child get chilled. Dry quickly and thoroughly. Take the temperature again. If necessary, repeat the bath routine. Try to reach the doctor again.

FRACTURES

☐ Call your doctor immediately.

☐ Until you receive instructions, do not move the child if she is reasonably comfortable.

☐ If the child must be moved, use a splint to keep the injured limb from moving.

☐ Apply an ice pack to reduce swelling.

HEAD INJURIES

■ If a child is unconscious or bleeding, call your doctor immediately. Control bleeding, but do not move the child.

☐ If a child is conscious, a cold compress will reduce swelling and pain of bruises. Call your doctor for further instructions.

NOSEBLEED

☐ Keep the child quiet and still. He can sit or lie down, but make sure the blood drains out rather than down the throat by having him lean forward slightly or lie on his side.

☐ With your thumb and forefinger, pinch the child's nose gently to stop the bleeding. Hold for five minutes by the clock, then check to see if it's still bleeding. Repeat if necessary.

☐ If the bleeding does not stop, call your doctor.

POISON (SWALLOWED)

■ Call the Poison Control Center immediately and follow their exact instructions. If you can't reach the center, call your doctor.

■ If you can't reach instant medical help on the phone and the child is conscious, give one or two glasses of milk (or water) to dilute the poison. Rush to the nearest hospital.

POISON OR CHEMICAL ON SKIN

■ Rinse with water immediately. Call your doctor.

POISON IVY, POISON OAK

■ After contact with plant, wash skin well with dishwashing liquid. Remove clothing and wash, also.

☐ If a rash develops, keep the child cool. (Sweating makes the itching worse.)

☐ To relieve itching, use cold compresses or give cool baths. Add a drying agent such as colloidal oatmeal (available at drugstores) to the bath to help dry up blisters. Ask your doctor about using nonprescription hydrocortisone creams.

☐ Consult your doctor in case of a severe rash.

PUNCTURE WOUNDS

☐ Control bleeding if necessary. (see "Cuts," pages 225–226.)

☐ Clean well with soap and water. Bandage.

☐ Call the pediatrician. A tetanus booster shot may be necessary.

SHOCK

☐ Always treat a child for shock if an injury is serious.

■ Shock symptoms: The child may be weak, cold, pale, sweaty, breathing quickly but shallowly or nauseous.

■ Treatment: Lay her down. Cover her lightly with a blanket. Keep her warm but do not allow her to become overheated. Put a pillow under her legs to raise them 10 to 12 inches.

☐ Stay with the child and comfort her. Do not give her anything to eat or drink.

☐ Call your pediatrician.

SPLINTERS

☐ Soak the skin in soapy water.

☐ Use tweezers cleaned with alcohol to remove the splinter.

☐ Wash the opening.

☐ If the splinter is too large or deep for you to remove, see your doctor.

SPRAINS

☐ Keep the child quiet and elevate the limb for at least a half hour to reduce swelling.

☐ Keep an ice pack on a sprain.

☐ Call your doctor. If there is pain and/or swelling, the injured limb should be examined by a doctor.

STINGS

☐ See "Bee or Other Insect Stings," page 220.

SWALLOWED SMALL OBJECTS

☐ See "Choking," pages 223–224.

Emergency Telephone Numbers

Keep copies of this list, with the emergency phone numbers filled in, at *each* telephone extension in your home.

You are at (address) _____

Phone number is _____

Directions to this house _____

_____

Police _____

Fire _____

Ambulance _____

Poison Control Center _____

Hospital _____

Taxi _____

Pediatrician _____

Ob/gyn _____

Family doctor _____

Drugstore _____

Mother's business _____

Father's business _____

Friends and
neighbors _____

_____

_____

_____

_____

Relatives _____

_____

Calling the Doctor

Make copies of this page and fill it in before you call the doctor. Information to have ready:

Age of child: _____

Weight of child: _____

Temperature
(indicate whether it is
rectal or axillary):   _____

Symptoms (vomiting,   _____
watery eyes, etc.):   _____
Sequence and duration   _____
of symptoms: _____

Appearance (pale,   _____
flushed, spotted, etc.):   _____
Location and exact   _____
appearance of any rash: _____

Treatment or medicine   _____
administered before calling: _____

Questions to ask: _____

_____

_____

Doctor's instructions:

_____

_____

_____

Keep these completed sheets in a file, and you'll be able to refer to them whenever necessary.

Your Child's Immunization Chart
and Health Record

Child's Name _____

Blood Type _____ Rh Factor _____

Allergies/Sensitivities _____

Special Medical Conditions _____

Health Insurance Co. _____ Policy No. _____

	DTP	Polio	MMR	Hepatitis B	Haemophilus	Tetanus-Diphtheria
Birth						
1–2 months						
2 months						
4 months						
6 months						
6–12 months						
12–15 months						
15 months						
15–18 months						
4–6 years						
11–12 years						
14–16 years						

Fill in date of immunization.

Adapted with permission of American Academy of Pediatrics, copyright © 1992.

Visits to Doctor			
Height	Weight	Comments, illness, treatment	Doctor

Baby-sitter Checklist

Use the following checklist for information that you'll want the sitter to know. Basic emergency phone numbers should be left *in writing* in the form of a copy of page 231. Write down as much of the following information as is appropriate. (Keep copies for future use.)

- Any special health problems the child might have.
- Child's schedule (mealtime, bedtime).
- Child's special fears (such as thunder).
- Child's special routines (such as leave night-light on, wind up music box before stories).
- Layout of house.
- Location of all first-aid supplies.
- Location of fuse box or circuit breaker and how it works.
- Location of flashlights.
- Location and operation of fire extinguisher.
- Operation of fire/smoke and burglar alarm.
- Fire escape routes.
- Stove operation, if necessary.
- Operation of TV, stereo, etc.
- Whereabouts and habits of pets.
- How door locks work and location of extra keys (in case a bathroom door gets locked, for instance).
- Expected deliveries or visitors.
- How to handle phone calls. Sitters should never give out your whereabouts or tell exactly when you are expected home. They should say you'll be home soon and ask for the caller's name and number.

Baby-sitter List

Have the names of your baby-sitters all in one place. If one
is not available, just call the next one on your list. It's also
helpful to put down what times they are free, such as "only
on Friday nights" or "weekday afternoons." It will save you
some calling time.

Name	Phone Number	When Available

My Own Tips: What Worked for Me

Use this space for recording your own special tips. Feel free, as you use this book, to write in it often, indicating which tips worked best for you. This annotated copy will be useful later on with other children, or it will make a unique gift for you to give to another parent.

_____

_____

_____

_____

_____

_____

_____

_____

Index

239